SELF-DETERMINATION
IN EAST TIMOR

INTERNATIONAL PEACE ACADEMY
OCCASIONAL PAPER SERIES

SELF-DETERMINATION IN EAST TIMOR

The United Nations, the Ballot, and International Intervention

Ian Martin

LYNNE
RIENNER
PUBLISHERS

BOULDER
LONDON

*Royalties from this publication go to the Ai-Kameli Trust, established in
the United Kingdom to provide financial support for East Timorese undertaking
academic and vocational training that will enable them to contribute to
the strengthening of East Timorese society.*

Published in the United States of America in 2001 by
Lynne Rienner Publishers, Inc.
1800 30th Street, Boulder, Colorado 80301
www.rienner.com

and in the United Kingdom by
Lynne Rienner Publishers, Inc.
3 Henrietta Street, Covent Garden, London WC2E 8LU

Library of Congress Cataloging-in-Publication Data
Martin, Ian, 1946–
    Self-determination in East Timor : the United Nations, the ballot, and international
intervention / Ian Martin.
        p. cm.—(International Peace Academy occasional paper series)
    Includes index.
    ISBN 1-58826-033-X (pb : alk. paper)
    1. Timor Timur (Indonesia)—International status.   2. United Nations—Indonesia—
Timor Timur.   3. Self-determination, National.   I. Title.   II. Series.
KZ4477.5.T56 M37 2001
341.26—dc21
                                                                                    2001019796

British Cataloguing in Publication Data
A Cataloguing in Publication record for this book
is available from the British Library.

Printed and bound in the United States of America

The paper used in this publication meets the requirements
of the American National Standard for Permanence of
Paper for Printed Library Materials Z39.48-1984.

5 4 3 2 1

To the people of East Timor
and
to the staff of UNAMET,
remembering those who were killed
because they were both

Contents

Foreword, David M. Malone   9
Map of East Timor   10

1 Introduction   11

2 The 5 May Agreements   15

3 Launching UNAMET   37

4 Preparing the Ballot   53

5 Reconciliation and the Laying Down of Arms   67

6 Looking Ahead   79

7 Ballot and Revenge   87

8 International Intervention   103

9 Conclusion   119

Appendixes
    1 List of Acronyms   133
    2 Chronology   135
    3 5 May Agreements   141

4 UN Security Council Resolution 1246, 11 June 1999   149
5 UN Security Council Resolution 1264, 15 September 1999   153
6 Electoral Commission Determination   157

Index   161
About This Publication   169
Other International Peace Academy Publications   170
The International Peace Academy   171

Foreword

David M. Malone

The International Peace Academy derives great pleasure and pride from the publication of this work by Ian Martin on the momentous events in and concerning East Timor during 1999, events in which he was a central participant. When Ian agreed to undertake this project, we encouraged him to produce a concise text of interest to the practitioner as well as to the academic world. His credentials and service in so many capacities in the past twenty years (not least as secretary-general of Amnesty International) qualify him uniquely for this task, which he has carried through magnificently. The UN community, those in capitals responsible for international peace, security, and development, the international financial institutions, and many others have much to learn from his firsthand account of a desperate tale, which, as I write in early 2001, is beginning to yield a promising ending as the formal independence of East Timor approaches.

We are privileged to sponsor this publication, which was generously funded by the Ford Foundation. With great admiration, we thank Ian for taking a considerable amount of time to develop this fascinating text when so many other duties called and when distance (he is now serving the UN as Deputy Special Representative of the Secretary-General in Asmara, Eritrea) created a variety of obstacles to its conclusion.

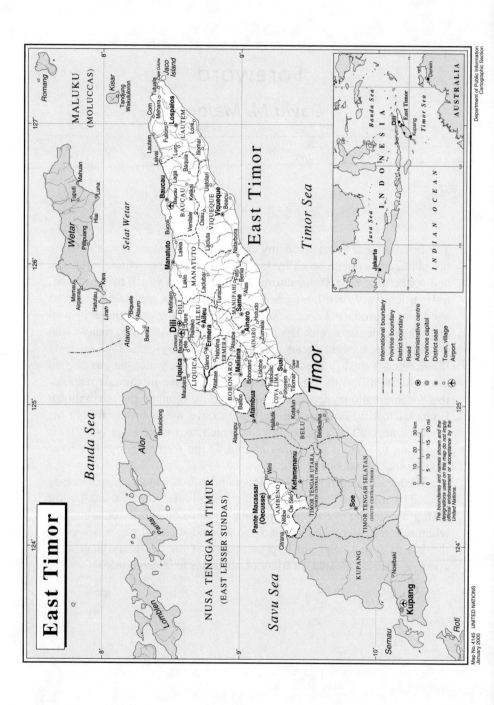

East Timor

Map No. 4145   UNITED NATIONS
January 2000

Department of Public Information
Cartographic Section

1

Introduction

At 9 P.M. on Friday 3 September 1999 in New York, Secretary-General Kofi Annan made his statement to the United Nations Security Council on the result of the East Timor Popular Consultation:

> On 5 May 1999, Portugal, Indonesia and the United Nations concluded an historic set of agreements intended to resolve the long-standing issue of East Timor. These 5 May Agreements requested me to determine, through a popular consultation based upon a universal, direct, and secret ballot, whether the East Timorese people would accept or reject a proposed special autonomy for East Timor within the unitary Republic of Indonesia.
>
> To enable me to fulfil this request, the United Nations Security Council established on 11 June 1999 the United Nations Mission in East Timor (UNAMET) which proceeded to organize and conduct the popular consultation. It registered 451,792 voters in East Timor and around the world, in a registration process which the Electoral Commission, a body composed of 3 independent commissioners, deemed to be a sound basis for the conduct of the consultation.
>
> Thus, on 30 August 1999, in a show of courage and determination, the people of East Timor turned out in massive numbers to vote in the popular consultation, expressing their will as to the future of the Territory. The votes cast have now been counted, and the Electoral Commission has assessed all outstanding complaints and certified the results of the popular consultation process. Therefore, in fulfillment of the task entrusted to me by the 5 May Agreements, I hereby announce that the result of the vote is 94,388, or 21.5 per cent, in *favor* and 344,580, or 78.5 per cent *against* the proposed special autonomy.

As the Secretary-General spoke in New York, it was the morning of Saturday 4 September in Dili, the capital of East Timor, and I was simultaneously making the same announcement at the press conference called by UNAMET. The press corps was already greatly reduced;

11

many of those who had intended to stay beyond the poll had left after postballot violence in Dili had included attacks on journalists. UNAMET local staff had much more reason to be apprehensive: two of their members were already known to have been murdered as the poll had closed in Ermera district, and two more had been killed as violence had erupted in the western town of Maliana, forcing the first withdrawal of UNAMET from one of its regional bases. The Secretary-General's personal phone calls to President B. J. Habibie urging Indonesia to fulfill its responsibility for maintaining security in East Timor, which it had insisted on retaining under the agreements, had been reinforced by the representations in Jakarta of the Secretary-General's Personal Representative for East Timor, Jamsheed Marker, as well as by those of key member states. But the announcement of the result of the ballot was the signal for violence to be unleashed across the territory, in which hundreds of people would be killed, buildings destroyed on a scale without precedent, and virtually an entire population displaced.

This violence provoked serious questions, in the minds of those of us who had sought to implement the agreements, as well as on the part of external critics of the UN. Had the agreements been so fundamentally flawed that they should never have been sanctioned by the UN and become the basis of the popular consultation? Was it right for the UN to go ahead with the ballot in security conditions that utterly failed to correspond to those that the UN had laid down at the time of the agreements? Why had the extent of the violence, of which there had been many threats and warnings, not been fully foreseen and preempted?

In addition to these questions are others: How did it come about that the people of East Timor were at last offered the opportunity to determine their own future when for decades the conventional wisdom of diplomats had been that full international recognition of Indonesia's incorporation of the territory was only a matter of time? How did the UN succeed in organizing a ballot acclaimed by international observers on a timescale that had widely been regarded as unrealistic and in security conditions that posed a continual threat? How did an international community still bitterly divided over the legitimacy of military intervention in Kosovo reach rapid consensus in mandating and launching military intervention to address the violence in East Timor with unprecedented speed?

In addressing these questions, I am disqualified by the personal responsibility I exercised, as Special Representative of the Secretary-General for the East Timor Popular Consultation, from being the objective historian of events in which I was centrally involved. With that responsibility, however, go others: to record for future historians events of which I have a particular knowledge, and to share reflections on lessons that may be learned from them.

This account is not a personal memoir; I kept no diary, although with the agreement of the Secretary-General I have been able to check the accuracy of my recollections against reports I submitted to UN headquarters and notes of meetings, as well as against the recollections of others. My account does not attempt to describe either the beauty of East Timor and the warmth of its people or the violence and devastation to which I was one witness. My aim is to offer an accurate account of events and my own analysis of them, not an evocation of the extraordinary atmosphere in which many of them occurred. I have used notes to cite some important sources and to direct the reader to accounts by other participants or observers; elsewhere I am relying on my own direct knowledge of events or a distillation of interviews with those with firsthand knowledge. As head of UNAMET, I was responsible for its overall assessments and recommendations; I have used the first person only where my own participation in events seemed to me to demand it.

I have been greatly aided by many other participants in these events. Jamsheed Marker, Francesc Vendrell, and Tamrat Samuel were central to the UN role regarding East Timor for many years, and they and others in the Secretariat shared their knowledge and perspectives with me before, during, and after my own involvement. I have had the benefit of the reflections of principal Indonesian and Portuguese participants in the negotiations and in subsequent events, including during visits to Jakarta and Lisbon. Senior policymakers and diplomats from other key member states were generous with their time—in New York, Canberra, Wellington, Tokyo, Washington, D.C., and London; they included those who participated in Security Council deliberations on East Timor and in its September 1999 mission to Jakarta and Dili. Civilian, police, and military colleagues from UNAMET have helped me to reconstruct and analyze our experience. A particular privilege of my role has been my access at different stages to the political and religious leaders of the East Timorese.

My own first engagement with East Timor came when I began working for Amnesty International in 1985. The role of nongovernmental organizations (NGOs), and of some remarkable individuals, who sustained concern for East Timor when the diplomatic world was at its most indifferent, is a story with important lessons, although it is not the story told here. Many of them have contributed greatly to my understanding.

I undertook much of the research for this book as a Visiting Fellow at the International Peace Academy (IPA), New York, and am most grateful to its president, David Malone, and his colleagues for welcoming me into the most stimulating environment that exists for someone who wants to return from the field to the center of current debates on the UN's work for peace. I also wish to thank the Ford Foundation for the grant to the IPA that supported my research, its publication, and its dissemination.

I believe that the achievement of self-determination for East Timor did great credit to the United Nations as an institution; without the UN, and without the principled persistence of committed individuals within it, a fundamental human right of the East Timorese might never have been realized. I do not conceal pride in the collective performance of UNAMET as a mission; its international and local staff conducted themselves with commitment and courage as well as professionalism. This is the account of a UN mission and its context; it cannot possibly do justice to the struggle of the East Timorese themselves, even during the period on which it focuses, let alone over the preceding twenty-four years. I wish to make clear, however, that the ultimate achievement belongs to the East Timorese people, whose sustained determination would not allow the international community to close the file on the denial of their right to self-determination, and whose determination in 1999 enabled and compelled UNAMET to carry through its task.

2

The 5 May Agreements

FROM PORTUGUESE TO INDONESIAN ADMINISTRATION

Until the change of government in Lisbon in April 1974, Portugal had considered East Timor, where it had begun to establish its colonial authority more than four centuries before, as its "overseas province." Rejecting that contention, the UN General Assembly declared in 1960 that the territories under Portuguese administration were non-self-governing territories within the meaning of Chapter XI of the UN Charter.

The "Carnation Revolution" in Portugal opened a new era for the Portuguese colonies. Portugal now acknowledged its Chapter XI obligations, and in July 1974 a constitutional law was adopted abrogating the former definition of an overseas province and accepting the right to self-determination, including independence, of the colonies. In July 1975, a law was passed providing for the formation of a transitional government in East Timor to prepare for the election of a popular assembly in 1976. It envisaged the termination of Portuguese sovereignty in October 1978.

East Timorese began to organize politically in preparation for their self-determination. In May 1974, the União Democrática Timorense (UDT; Timorese Democratic Union) and the Associação Social Democrática Timor (ASDT; Timorese Social Democratic Association), which later changed its name to Frente Revolucionária de Timor Leste Independente (Fretilin; Revolutionary Front for an Independent East Timor), were formed. The former advocated continued association with Portugal before independence, while the latter favored immediate independence. The most significant among a number of smaller parties, the

Associação Popular Democrática Timorense (Apodeti; Timorese Popular Democratic Association), favored eventual integration of East Timor as an autonomous province within Indonesia. In June 1975, a conference convened by Portugal in Macau to discuss a gradual decolonization plan was boycotted by Fretilin, while UDT and Apodeti attended. Fretilin objected to the invitation of Apodeti, which it claimed was supported by certain factions in Indonesia.

In January 1975, UDT and Fretilin formed a coalition with independence as the common objective. The alliance was short-lived, however. A rift developed between the two parties as Fretilin appeared increasingly left-wing and UDT moved closer to Indonesia. The coalition collapsed in May, and during the second half of 1975 the situation rapidly escalated to open hostilities and civil war. In August, the Portuguese governor and administration left the mainland and withdrew to the island of Atauro. Covert Indonesian special forces began operating across the border with West Timor. On 28 November 1975, Fretilin, which was reported to be in control of most of the territory, relying on the loyalty of many who were in the Portuguese local military forces and on weapons left by the Portuguese, declared the independence of East Timor and the establishment of the Democratic Republic of East Timor. On 30 November 1975, a coalition of pro-Indonesian parties (mainly UDT and Apodeti) also proclaimed the independence of the territory and its integration with Indonesia.

Indonesia had always denied any territorial claim to East Timor, which had never been part of the Dutch East Indies. But on 7 December 1975, Indonesia launched a naval, air, and land invasion of East Timor. The pro-Indonesian parties declared the establishment of the Provisional Government of East Timor, and as the Indonesian military campaign against Fretilin's resistance led to increased territorial control, they purported to establish a Regional Popular Assembly. On 31 May 1976, at its only meeting, this assembly decided to petition Indonesia to formally integrate East Timor. The UN General Assembly's Special Committee of Twenty-Four (Decolonization Committee) declined the invitation of the Indonesian government to attend the meeting of the assembly and to visit East Timor. Among other things, it cited its obligation to be guided by relevant General Assembly resolutions and the fact that it had in no way been involved in the proceedings leading up to the meeting of the assembly.

On 17 July 1976, President Suharto of Indonesia promulgated Law 7/76 providing for the integration of East Timor into Indonesia as its twenty-seventh province. Indonesia thereafter maintained that by the act of the assembly, the people of East Timor had exercised their right to self-determination and had become independent through integration with Indonesia. The United Nations neither recognized the authority of the Regional Popular Assembly nor endorsed its decision concerning the status of the territory. Portugal never relinquished its authority as administering power of the territory. It wrote into its constitution the commitment that "Portugal shall remain bound by its responsibility, in accordance with international law, to promote and safeguard the right to self-determination and independence of Timor Leste," giving its president specific responsibility to achieve this aim. Fretilin continued to resist the integration of East Timor into Indonesia through its armed wing, the Forças Armadas de Libertação Nacional de Timor-Leste (Falintil; Armed Forces for the National Liberation of East Timor).

The early years of the conflict resulted in heavy loss of life. Estimates of the number who died as a result of the conflict, including the famine and disease that accompanied the displacement of large parts of the population, range from tens of thousands, acknowledged by Indonesia itself, to as many as 200,000. Extensive human rights violations were committed by the Indonesian armed forces against pro-independence activists and their suspected supporters. They received little attention from the international community until, in November 1991, Indonesian security forces opened fire on a pro-independence demonstration of mourners near the Santa Cruz cemetery in Dili, killing a large number of people (estimates ranged from the official 50 to well over 200). The television images and reports produced by journalists present at the scene had a major impact on international opinion. The 1992 capture of resistance leader José Alexandre "Xanana" Gusmão, who in 1993 was sentenced to life imprisonment (later reduced to twenty years), and his continued activism from prison, raised his profile and that of the resistance. In 1996, the Nobel Peace Prize was awarded to two leading East Timorese personalities, Bishop Carlos Filipe Ximenes Belo, the apostolic administrator of Dili, and José Ramos-Horta, the leading exiled spokesman of the East Timorese resistance, "for their work toward a just and peaceful solution to the conflict in East Timor." A growing number of nongovernmental and parliamentary groups in Western countries began to influence the policies of their governments in the direction of supporting self-determination for East Timor.

THE UNITED NATIONS AND
THE QUESTION OF EAST TIMOR

On 22 December 1975 and 22 April 1976, the Security Council had adopted Resolutions 384 (1975) and 389 (1976), calling on Indonesia to withdraw without delay all its forces from the territory, and on all states to respect the territorial integrity of East Timor and the people's right to self-determination. From then until 1981, the General Assembly passed annual resolutions reaffirming the inalienable right of the East Timorese to self-determination and expressing concern at the suffering of the civilian population.

In its Resolution 37/30 (1982), the General Assembly gave the Secretary-General the mandate to begin a diplomatic effort to help find a comprehensive solution to the problem. Thereafter, while the question of East Timor remained on the agenda of the assembly, consideration of the item was deferred each year on the basis of the progress report submitted by the Secretary-General on his good offices on the question. There continued to be annual discussion of East Timor in the Decolonization Committee, and the Santa Cruz killings stirred the Commission on Human Rights into some activity.

The direct discussions between Indonesia and Portugal, which began in July 1983 under the auspices of the Secretary-General, saw little progress for well over a decade. In 1986, Portugal, encouraged by the UN and pressured by its European partners, came close to agreeing that East Timorese participation, with UN observation, in the Indonesian elections scheduled for 1987 would be treated as an expression of the wishes of the population of the territory. However, after internal debate, the Portuguese government reasserted an insistence on a proper act of self-determination. Thereafter, discussions focused on a proposed visit by a Portuguese parliamentary delegation, which finally failed in 1991. From 1992, the human rights situation commanded increased attention, with eventual agreement in 1994 on access to East Timor for the UN and human rights and humanitarian organizations. The UN worked to bring together East Timorese leaders who could eventually constitute a consultative group, and the first meeting in 1995 of the All-Inclusive Intra–East Timorese Dialogue (AIETD) led to a focus on preserving and promoting East Timor's cultural identity.

A new Secretary-General brought fresh determination to the UN's efforts. Soon after he took office, Secretary-General Kofi Annan decided to attempt to revitalize the tripartite process, and in February 1997 he appointed Ambassador Jamsheed Marker of Pakistan as his Personal Representative (PRSG) for East Timor. The UN role became increasingly proactive, with visits to Indonesia, Portugal, and East Timor itself.

POLITICAL CHANGE IN INDONESIA AND EAST TIMOR

It was the momentous political changes that began to take place in Indonesia with the fall of President Suharto in May 1998 that opened the way for significant progress on the diplomatic front. In June 1998, the successor government of President Habibie stated that it was prepared to give East Timor a wide-ranging autonomy, with Jakarta retaining only three areas: foreign affairs, external defense, and some aspects of monetary and fiscal policy. In August 1998, during their meeting with the Secretary-General, the foreign ministers of Indonesia and Portugal reached agreement that their senior officials should begin in-depth discussions on a possible wide-ranging autonomy for East Timor, without prejudice to their respective positions of principle. In effect, they agreed to put aside, for the time being, the question of the final status of East Timor and to attempt to define the parameters of a suitable autonomy. While for Indonesia this autonomy would be the final dispensation, Portugal was willing to consider autonomy only as an interim or transitional arrangement pending the eventual exercise by the people of East Timor of their right to self-determination. The East Timorese resistance, under the leadership of Xanana Gusmão, had for some years endorsed the idea of transitional arrangements within Indonesia for an agreed period before the holding of a referendum.

Indonesia had always resisted any direct involvement of East Timorese political leaders in the negotiations, maintaining the position that the East Timorese had expressed their will once and for all in 1976 and that the international issue was kept alive only by the unreasonable obstinacy of Portugal. Its acquiescence in the UN's convening of the annual All-Inclusive Intra–East Timorese Dialogue, which began in 1995, had been on the condition that this dialogue did not address the political status of East Timor. It now found that a number of former adherents of integration had become disillusioned with Indonesian rule and were advocating self-determination and that the generation who had grown up and been educated under Indonesian rule were even more disaffected than their parents. The independence movement itself became more broadly united with the formation in April 1998 of the National Council of Timorese Resistance (CNRT), under the leadership of Gusmão. The UN and others urged the release of Gusmão and the establishment out of the AIETD of a more active group of East Timorese leaders who could develop an East Timorese position on a formula for a settlement. Indonesia maintained that Gusmão would be released only as part of an overall settlement, but in August 1998 agreed that the East Timorese would be more closely associated with the tripartite process, primarily through the UN.

In East Timor itself, the mood of growing political freedom throughout Indonesia was reflected in increasingly open pro-independence activism, which rapidly challenged the control of the authorities. Large pro-independence crowds came out during a visit of European

Union ambassadors in June 1998, and security personnel opened lethal fire in East Timor's second city, Baucau. Indonesian migrants in East Timor had been feeling increasingly insecure, and a trickle of departures became a flood as some were subjected to attacks. Paramilitary groups of pro-integration East Timorese had long existed, but in late 1998, new groups began to be established to contest the assertiveness of pro-independence campaigning. Killings of soldiers and the seizure of army weapons by Falintil and independence supporters in the town of Alas (Manufahi district) in November 1998 gave rise to military retaliation in which civilians were killed and many more displaced. The visits of PRSG Marker and other UN representatives were attended by a determination of pro-independence youth to demonstrate and corresponding nervousness on the part of the Indonesian authorities. Gusmão's appeals from his Jakarta prison for calm on the part of his student supporters became less certain to be heeded.

THE SECOND OPTION

Governments with some of the closest and most influential relationships with Indonesia welcomed the initiatives of the Habibie government, including the release of many political prisoners and the offer of special autonomy for East Timor. But they realized that this offer, combined with Indonesia's reluctance to deal directly with the East Timorese independence leadership, would not be enough to resolve the issue. Meanwhile, they saw the situation on the ground in East Timor slipping rapidly beyond the control of the Indonesian authorities, and perhaps beyond the control of responsible East Timorese leadership.

Australia, under governments of both its major parties, had been the nation most firmly committed to the integration of East Timor with Indonesia. At the end of 1978, eager to settle the seabed border between Australia and East Timor (the "Timor Gap"), Australia had gone beyond the de facto recognition extended by a number of governments and announced that it would grant de jure recognition to Indonesia's claimed sovereignty when talks on delineating the seabed boundary began.[1] In opposition, however, the Australian Labor Party began to reconsider its policy and in August 1997 espoused East Timor's right to self-determination. Against the backdrop of the dramatic changes in Indonesia, the government of Prime Minister John Howard began its own policy review.[2] In August 1998, Australian government officials, picking up a suggestion of Marker's, canvased a range of views of East Timorese in East Timor, Indonesia, and elsewhere and found "negligible acceptance" that East Timorese should concede to the precondition of accepting international recognition of integration in return for autonomy. All those consulted believed that there was a need for the East Timorese to be closely engaged in the process of negotiation. The Australian government, shared its report of these views with Indonesia and the UN, whose own assessment it confirmed. Then on 19 December 1998, Howard sent Habibie a letter that reflected this assessment. He emphasized that Australia continued to maintain its long-standing position that "the interests of Australia, Indonesia and East Timor are best served by East Timor remaining part of Indonesia." The issue, he urged, could be resolved only through direct negotiations between Indonesia and East Timorese leaders. A decisive element of East Timorese opinion was insisting on an act of self-determination:

> It might be worth considering, therefore, a means of addressing the East Timorese desire for an act of self-determination in a manner that avoids an early and final decision on the future status of the province. One way of doing this would be to build into the autonomy package a review mechanism along the lines of the Matignon Accords in New Caledonia. The Matignon Accords have enabled a compromise political solution to be implemented while deferring a referendum on the final status of New Caledonia for many years. The successful implementation of an autonomy package with a built-in review mechanism would allow time to convince the East Timorese of the benefits of autonomy within the Indonesian Republic.[3]

This letter was not well received by Habibie when it was presented to him by the Australian ambassador in Jakarta on 23 December. He took exception to the apparent colonial analogy with New Caledonia. But when the letter reached him for a second time, on the arrival of the original from Canberra in January, he used it to instruct his ministers to consider a new option. He sent copies of the letter on to them with a handwritten instruction to consider a change of policy, later remembered by his adviser: if the East Timorese, after twenty-five years of being treated as being a full part of Indonesia, still feel that they cannot be fully integrated into Indonesia, isn't it democratic and just that we should separate in peace?[4]

On 27 January 1999, the minister for information emerged from a cabinet meeting to announce that if the East Timorese decided to reject the offer of special autonomy, the president would recommend to the People's Consultative Assembly that the July 1976 law integrating East Timor as Indonesia's twenty-seventh province should be revoked. Soon after, Gusmão was moved from Cipinang prison to a prison house, where he was more readily able to receive international and East

Timorese visitors and play an active role in the accelerating politics and diplomacy.

The announcement of what came to be called "the second option" involves two intriguing issues: How crucial were the change in Australia's position and the Howard letter in giving rise to Habibie's new proposal, and how readily or reluctantly did the Indonesian cabinet adopt it?

The fact that the offer of special autonomy alone would not resolve the issue was increasingly obvious from reports of the situation in East Timor, and its acknowledgment was being quietly pressed on Indonesia by Marker and by other governments besides Australia, most notably the United States and the European Union. Indonesia's economic negotiators were anxious for a resolution, and even within the Indonesian armed forces there was a growing desire to be rid of the problem. The possibility of East Timor's independence had become a subject of open discussion in Indonesia, with several opposition figures and nongovernmental actors (and in private some civilian and military officials) foreseeing the holding of an eventual referendum. Habibie himself had no personal stake in East Timor, and some of his closest advisers from the more liberal wing of Ikatan Cendekiawan Muslim se-Indonesia (Indonesian Association of Muslim Intellectuals), which he had chaired, were among those who questioned Indonesia's interest in retaining the territory, with its overwhelmingly Christian population. As an interim successor to Suharto, whose democratic legitimacy was open to challenge, Habibie was eager to impress the international community with his commitment to democracy and human rights. He also saw a settlement of the long-standing issue of East Timor as a potential springboard to his election as president in his own right. A further development in Indonesian policy was therefore in the logic of the situation. But the fact that Australia had been the firmest supporter of the integration of East Timor made its conversion to self-determination of special significance and explains at least in part the bitterness that was to enter its relationship with Indonesia.

Habibie's January proposal undoubtedly took his cabinet colleagues by surprise, but it was discussed in cabinet committee and then in cabinet without opposition, despite misgivings. Foreign Minister Ali Alatas and his senior negotiators were approaching the end of the negotiation of the special autonomy proposal and regarded any further change of position as premature, at best. Most surprising in retrospect is the lack of opposition from the minister for defense and head of the armed forces, General Wiranto, or from his predecessor, Feisal Tanjung, who as coordinating minister for political and security affairs chaired the cabinet committee that considered the change in policy before the full cabinet and would oversee its implementation. But Wiranto and most of those at the head of the armed forces since Wiranto ousted Suharto's son-in-law, Lieutenant-General Prabowo Subianto, were not among the generals who had the greatest stake in East Timor. His expressed reservations were confined to the concern that the legitimacy of the role of the armed forces in the territory since 1975 should not be called into question.[5]

The lack of expressed opposition may have been due in part to the degree of authority habitually accorded to the position of president, and to the fact that Habibie, while respecting the process of cabinet consideration, had clearly made up his own mind. More important, perhaps, the eventual outcome of the ballot should not give rise to an underestimation of the belief in Jakarta, which prevailed long after the January decision, that a majority of East Timorese would opt to remain with Indonesia—or could be induced to do so.

The timetable for Habibie's second option, with his insistence on an immediate choice before the People's Consultative Assembly met at the end of August, was an alternative to what was being pressed upon the Indonesian government much more than it was an acceptance of it. Only the more radical campaigners in East Timor were urging on Indonesia an immediate decision on independence. Gusmão remained uncompromising in his demand for an eventual referendum and his objective of independence but was prepared to be very flexible in defining an extended period of transition before a referendum, in which Indonesia would continue to play an active role. He spoke publicly and privately about creating an atmosphere "in which the military would not feel defeated, but rather participants in the process,"[6] and of his concern to lay the basis for friendly relations between Indonesia and an independent East Timor. His New Year message for 1999 defended the CNRT's acceptance of transitional autonomy, against those demanding an immediate referendum, as a means of achieving national reconciliation and a solution that would be long-lasting.[7] Bishop Belo's longstanding advocacy of a referendum, which had been consistent since he had written to UN Secretary-General Javier Pérez de Cuéllar in 1989, was also coupled with a keen awareness of the risk of violent conflict and need for a period of transition.[8] The Australian survey of East Timorese views had found the clear majority view to be a transitional autonomy arrangement to be followed by a referendum or similar process after a specified period, varying among the respondents from three to twenty years. Such a transition was the maximum being advocated by any of the concerned governments, and Portugal would have endorsed such an outcome had it been acceptable to the East Timorese. In the negotiations, the UN had suggested autonomy with international supervision for five to seven years, with early agreement on a mechanism for ascertaining the views of the East Timorese at the end of that period. The Howard letter explicitly advocated a course of action that "*avoids* an early and final decision on the future status of the province" (emphasis added).

Questioned about Indonesia's objection to the idea of transitional autonomy pending a later referendum, Alatas asked why, if the East Timorese did not want autonomy, Indonesia should be asked to continue to bear the burden of East Timor's financing and of "all kinds of accusations if anything went wrong"?[9] Later he would describe the spirit of Habibie's response to the international pressure more fully, in a retrospective interview soon after he left the office of foreign minister. He recalled how the proposal for wide-ranging autonomy in mid-1998 was initially well received:

> We started negotiations, but then we were attacked, we were criticized by East Timorese who are against us, also by certain NGOs and certain governments, saying your proposal is not enough, they will never accept it. Or they'd say that it is only acceptable if after five years to 10 years you still give them a referendum. You give them your wide-ranging autonomy, you still give them all these things, you continue to pay for them, and after five to 10 years they'd still have the opportunity to say goodbye and thank you very much. It was no wonder that *Pak* Habibie then said that maybe we need an alternative. If our proposal is indeed unacceptable, I am not going to give alternatives in which they ask five to 10 years and then a referendum. Our proposal was that if they reject it, then let's pack and leave. Everybody was shocked, but that was the idea of the best solution.[10]

THE MILITIA RESPONSE

Among those who were most shocked were elements of the Indonesian armed forces and Indonesia's supporters in East Timor. The operation of paramilitary groups had long been a feature of Indonesian control of the population. In late 1998 and early 1999, long-established paramilitary groups such as Halilintar (Thunderbolt, in Bobonaro district), Tim Saka (Baucau), and Tim Alfa (Lautem) were joined by new ones, including Besi Merah Putih (Iron Red and White—the colors of the Indonesian flag—Liquiça), Mati Hidup Demi Integrasi or Mahidi (Live or Die for the Sake of Integration, Ainaro), Laksaur (Cova Lima), and Aitarak (Thorn, Dili). Already before the announcement of the second option, they had begun to move against independence supporters. Following the announcement, they went on the rampage. From January to April, gross human rights violations were committed, with independence activists and presumed supporters seized, tortured, and ill treated; in some cases activists were killed, many homes were destroyed, and inhabitants were displaced.[11] The CNRT leadership, which had only openly declared itself and established offices from September 1998, was rapidly driven underground again.[12] In the climate of immediate and future insecurity, the outflow of Indonesian settlers and professionals increased, with serious consequences for medical services, the education system, and commerce.

Observers had little doubt that the Indonesian armed forces (the TNI) were responsible for forming and arming the pro-integration militia groups and for directing their activities.[13] While this was officially denied to international critics, there was no concealment of the degree of official approval of their existence: military, police, and civilian officials attended inaugural and other functions throughout the territory. The culmination was a parade ceremony in front of the governor's office in Dili on 17 April, in the presence of senior officials, at which João Tavares of Halilintar and Eurico Guterres of Aitarak spoke as commander and deputy commander respectively of the militias' umbrella organization.

The worst of the killings—indeed the worst massacre since Santa Cruz in 1991—occurred in Liquiça on 6 April 1999. Some 2,000 people had sought shelter in the church compound after violent incidents in and around the town in preceding days in which civilians had been killed by Besi Merah Putih (BMP) militia and Indonesian military. According to the investigation established after the popular consultation by the Indonesian National Human Rights Commission (Komnas HAM), BMP militia supported by the district military command attacked those who had taken refuge, killing approximately thirty people; other estimates of the dead are considerably higher.[14] A wave of international protest did nothing to check the militia offensive, as killings continued in several districts. At the mass gathering of pro-integration militia and supporters in front of the governor's office in Dili on 17 April, Aitarak commander Eurico Guterres ordered "all pro-integration militias to conduct a cleansing of all those who betrayed integration. . . . Capture and kill if you need."[15] Later that day, BMP and Aitarak militia attacked the homes of pro-independence leaders. Well over a hundred people who had fled from Liquiça and elsewhere had sought protection in the house of Manuel Carrascalão, a former supporter of integration who had become a critic of Indonesian administration and an advocate of a referendum; at least fifteen people were killed, including Carrascalão's son, when the house was attacked.[16]

The timing of these bloody events seemed calculated to derail the tripartite negotiations. Forewarned that the 17 April parade in Dili would be the occasion for further violence, Marker had summoned the Indonesian permanent representative in New York the previous day and given him a copy of the handbill the militia were distributing. It was to no avail. Irish foreign minister David Andrews, visiting Dili that day, personally witnessed the "unconcern" and inaction of the East Timor military commander, Colonel Tono Suratman, in the face of appeals from Carrascalão regarding events of which Suratman was clearly fully aware; Andrews reported them directly to Habibie and Alatas.[17]

THE LAST PHASE OF NEGOTIATIONS

The progress on the diplomatic front had meanwhile been in positive contrast to the deterioration in the situation in East Timor. In October 1998, the UN had submitted to Indonesia and Portugal a proposed constitutional framework for self-administration for either a permanent or a transitional autonomy, drawn up with the assistance of an international legal expert. This framework elaborated on first ideas offered by the UN as a basis for discussion in April 1998, which had promptly been circulated and misrepresented in East Timor as a UN proposal indicating that the organization favored autonomy within Indonesia. The draft was refined in tripartite discussions and through UN consultations with East Timorese leaders, including Gusmão. By early February 1999, the foreign ministers had resolved most issues, with final consultations to be held with their respective governments.

The announcement of the second option had, however, changed the context for the negotiation. Since Indonesia was offering the East Timorese the opportunity to reject autonomy, Portugal felt that it could not object to whatever the Indonesian government would finally decide regarding the nature of its offer. Alatas, who wanted an autonomy arrangement that he felt could be attractive to the East Timorese, faced wider concerns in Jakarta at the possible implications for autonomy demands from other Indonesian provinces, requiring a significant watering-down of the framework.[18] In April, the autonomy draft was finalized with the incorporation of the amendments required by Jakarta.

The principles of the final autonomy framework remained that Indonesia would retain responsibility for foreign affairs, defense, currency, and finance. An East Timorese Regional Council would legislate in other areas, elect the governor, and recommend members of the advisory board of the government of the Special Autonomous Region of East Timor (SARET). East Timor would have its own police and judiciary. The TNI would retain a presence for external security and could be deployed outside their bases in the event of an external armed attack, or imminent threat of such an attack, without consultation with the regional authorities. The region would remain subject to Indonesian national monetary and fiscal policies, and to national taxation, while having competence over local taxation. Natural resources would be under the control of the regional government, except those considered to be strategic or vital under Indonesian national laws. An initial proposal that East Timor have its own citizenship, with control over settlement of non–East Timorese Indonesian citizens and the entry of non-Indonesians, was replaced by a definition of East Timorese "identity," with immigration control remaining in the hands of the central government. The Indonesian flag would continue to fly, and the SARET would have its own coat of arms. The governor would be elected by the Regional Council from a list of candidates previously approved by the president of Indonesia and subject to his formal confirmation after election. The East Timorese courts would be subject to the Supreme Court of Indonesia as court of final appeal. Indonesian concern for coordination between the regional and central governments was reflected in a series of provisions, including the presence of a senior central government official in Dili and assistance from the Indonesian National Police to the police force of the SARET "in exceptional cases." Provision for Portugal to have an office in East Timor was dropped, but the UN Secretary-General would have the responsibility and authority to monitor and verify compliance with the agreement and to establish offices in East Timor, within a specific timeframe subject to further agreement.

In the context of the Indonesian perspective that East Timor was only one of a number of its provinces with separatist or autonomy claims, Indonesia's concern regarding the precedent the proposed framework might set for others was understandable. It is unlikely that the precise degree of autonomy offered was going to be the determining factor for many East Timorese when they came to choose between autonomy and independence. But the limitations placed on autonomy in the final framework were quickly criticized by East Timorese activists, and would certainly not maximize the prospects of its acceptance.[19]

As soon as Indonesia had decided to offer the second option, the key issue became the manner of consultation. The UN identified three possibilities: a direct ballot for or against the autonomy proposal; an indirect ballot in which the East Timorese would elect a representative council, which in turn would consider and decide whether to accept the autonomy proposal or proceed toward independence; or an informal consultation, expanding the canvasing of the views of East Timorese leaders, in which the UN was already involved. For a time, the UN and Gusmão, both expecting Indonesian rejection of a direct ballot, saw advantages in the election of a representative council; this would avoid the risks of a referendum, while bringing into existence a body of East Timorese with democratic legitimacy that might serve as an interim assembly under either outcome. But when the ministers met with the Secretary-General in March, to the surprise of both the UN and Portugal, there was rapid agreement on a direct, UN-administered ballot for or against the autonomy proposal. For Portugal, there could be no democratic consultation that was not universal. Alatas too saw this as the best means to an outcome not subject to further challenge. He continued to reject the term "referendum," which was the demand of the independence campaigners and associated with everything most unacceptable to Indonesian hard-liners. It implied an act of self-determination, whereas in the Indonesian view, East Timor had been integrated by decision of its Majelis Permusyawaratan Rakyat (MPR; Peoples Consultative Assembly); any change in its status would be by decision of the MPR in the light of the "consultation." Alatas was also concerned that those outside East Timor should be consulted where they were living and not required or encouraged to return to East Timor to take part in a referendum; this would become an issue when Ramos-Horta proposed to return before the ballot. The agreements therefore used the expression "popular consultation," and the form of question to be put to the East Timorese respected the Indonesian position: "Do you *accept* the proposed special autonomy for East Timor within the Unitary State of the Republic of Indonesia?" or "Do you *reject* the proposed special autonomy for East Timor, leading to East Timor's separation from Indonesia?"

Once the Portuguese had achieved the key objective of a UN-administered universal ballot, they were not inclined to hold up or threaten an agreement over other aspects of the arrangements, many of which became matters for the UN. Immediately after the March negotiating session, the UN sent an assessment mission to East Timor, headed by the director of the Asia and Pacific Division of its Department of Political Affairs, Francesc Vendrell, who was Marker's deputy throughout the negotiations. It included a senior electoral expert and enabled the UN's Electoral Assistance Division to develop detailed proposals for the modalities of the consultation for the next session, in April. Alatas was under pressure to conclude an agreement, as the timetable was of crucial importance to Habibie. Indonesia's elections would be held on 7 June, and the new MPR was expected to convene at the end of August and then to proceed to elect a new president. Alatas was therefore required to conclude an agreement that would specify a ballot by mid-August. On most issues, the negotiations were ripe for final agreement when the ministers were to meet again in April.

SECURITY AND THE 5 MAY AGREEMENTS

What was to prove the most crucial issue, however, had yet to be addressed in the negotiations: the security arrangements. It had been increasingly preoccupying the UN. The political affairs officer long responsible for East Timor, who had most often visited the territory, Tamrat Samuel, reported from visits in December 1998 and February 1999 on the rapidly deteriorating human rights and security situation. He proposed the formation of local conflict management bodies in East Timor, involving the church, military, police, local administration, and pro-independence and pro-integration activists. All the East Timorese parties, including the pro-integrationists, agreed to participate. Gusmão was thinking along similar lines. The proposal for a peace commission or commissions was supported by Bishop Belo, pressed by Marker with the Indonesians, and positively received by Alatas, but the military were reluctant. Bishop Belo and Gusmão were eager for the UN to establish an immediate presence in East Timor to help calm the situation, but the Indonesian position was that this would be negotiated as part of an agreement and could not precede it.

As it became clear that the consultation would take the form of a ballot, the UN considered the security arrangements and the nature of the international presence that would accompany it. Vendrell's assessment mission, which was in East Timor in late March, reported on the dangerous level of tension and political violence, which risked becoming unmanageable in the period prior to and after the consultation unless the military adopted a neutral stand and disarmed or otherwise neutralized the militia. It recommended requiring the absolute neutrality of the Indonesian army and police; the disarmament of all paramilitary groups and militia; the withdrawal of some Indonesian forces and restrictions on the movement of others, matched by similar restraint on Falintil forces; and the maintenance of law and order solely by the police. It envisaged a small group of international civilian police to advise the local law enforcement authorities, as well as the immediate establishment of the proposed Peace Commission.

The murderous events in Liquiça and Dili in April brought the security situation to a new level of international concern. Gusmão's orders to Falintil had been to refrain from any action, and since the Alas events of November 1998, this discipline had largely been respected, despite militia killings and other abuses against pro-independence civilians. When the first killings in Liquiça came immediately after the Bali-based commander of the military region that included East Timor, Major-General Adam Damiri, openly endorsed the militia and acknowledged army provision of arms and training, Gusmão decided he could no longer fail to respond.[20] On 5 April he issued a statement declaring:

> I now wish to inform the international community that the situation has reached an intolerable limit in East Timor. Therefore, I am compelled to authorize the Falintil guerillas to undertake all necessary action in defense of the population of East Timor against the unprovoked and murderous attacks of armed civilian groups and ABRI.[21] In response to the numerous appeals from the People of East Timor, I also authorize a general popular insurrection against the armed militia groups who have been killing the population with impunity under the indifferent eye of the international community.[22]

The international community, horrified that the successful conclusion of an agreement was imperiled, responded with pressure on Gusmão to maintain restraint and with intensified expressions of concern to Jakarta. Alatas assured Marker that Wiranto had at last been persuaded to agree to the formation of a peace commission. Yet these responses failed to prevent the further killings in Dili on 17 April. The highest profile among renewed government representations was taken by Australia. Howard announced after telephoning Habibie that the latter had given fresh instructions to the Indonesian security forces, was determined to go ahead with the popular consultation, and had proposed a meeting between the two heads of government and their foreign ministers.

On 21 April, Wiranto presided over the signing of an agreement in Dili to cease hostilities and establish what was now called the Commission on Peace and Stability (KPS). A body that the UN and Gusmão had envisaged being convened by the UN itself under the auspices of the bishops was headed off into a body that would appear a TNI initiative and be tightly controlled by it. The Indonesian National Human Rights Commission, Komnas HAM, was brought in—against the better judgment of some of its members—to convene the KPS. The two representatives of CNRT/Falintil were balanced by two pro-integrationists, these being defined as the parties to the conflict, and then greatly outnumbered by the other members: the army, police, and local government. Not only the UN itself, but also the student and civil society representation it had envisaged, were excluded. While Gusmão gave his consent from his prison house in Jakarta, the only CNRT representative present at the signing, Leandro Isaac, was brought from the Dili police station, where he had taken refuge after his own house had been attacked.

It was in this heightened climate that the tripartite negotiations resumed for what was hoped to be their final session on 22 April. The UN presented its proposed security arrangements. In addition to the requirement of neutrality of the army and police, they included:

- All paramilitary groups and militia forces must be disarmed by the Indonesian Security Forces in a verifiable manner before the start of the consultation campaign.
- Prior to the start of the registration process, Indonesia should undertake a substantial and verifiable reduction of its military presence in East Timor. One month before the date of the consultation, the remaining troops will be confined to designated areas and the Indonesian police will be solely responsible for the maintenance of law and order.
- One month before the consultation, the Falintil forces will be confined to designated areas in preparation for their demobilization and reintegration into civilian society.
- The UN will make available a number of civilian police officers to act as advisers to the Indonesian police in the discharge of their duties and, at the time of the consultation, to supervise the escort of ballot papers and boxes to and from the polling sites.

In the negotiations, Alatas refused to agree to the inclusion of the specific UN proposals. A draft security annex to the main agreement retained the commitment to neutrality of the TNI and police, the maintenance of law and order solely by the police, and an advisory role for the United Nations Civilian Police (CIVPOL). But it made no reference to the withdrawal or restriction of the TNI and subsumed the crucial issue of the militia under a general reference to the role of the Commission on Peace and Stability: "The Commission, in cooperation with the United Nations, will elaborate a code of conduct, by which all parties should abide, for the period prior to and following the consultation, ensure the laying down of arms and take the necessary steps to achieve disarmament." It was written in that the Secretary-General would ascertain that the necessary security situation existed for the peaceful implementation of the consultation process prior to the start of registration.

The contrast between the weakness of this aspect of the proposed agreement and the actual situation in East Timor gave rise to expressions of dismay by the CNRT. Gusmão and Ramos-Horta urged that the presence of the TNI must be reduced to a thousand, the TNI and Falintil confined to designated areas, the paramilitary and militias disarmed, and security provided by an armed UN police force. The Portuguese sought to reopen the text they had agreed to only days before. The concern was shared within the UN Secretariat itself.[23] Referring to his responsibility under the draft annex to determine that the necessary security conditions existed for the start of the consultation process, the Secretary-General set out in a letter to Habibie the main elements that would need to be in place for him to do so. The Indonesians refused to accept the letter. The UN's requirements were therefore presented to the parties in a memorandum. They included the bringing of armed civilian groups under strict control and the prompt arrest and prosecution of those who incite or threaten to use violence; a ban on rallies by armed groups while ensuring the freedom of association and expression of all political forces and tendencies; the redeployment of Indonesian military forces; and the immediate institution of a process of laying down of arms by all armed groups to be completed well in advance of the holding of the ballot. The nature of redeployment of Indonesian military forces was unspecified, but the UN should participate fully in the Commission on Peace and Stability where such issues would be addressed.

No attempt was made in the negotiations to extend the role of CIVPOL beyond an advisory one, but the heightened concern argued for an increase in the numbers well beyond the fifty recommended by the UN's assessment mission. Formally this was a matter to be determined by the Secretary-General, subject to Security Council approval, but the meeting between Habibie and Howard, which took place in Bali on 27 April, was used to obtain Habibie's agreement that the number could go up to 300.[24]

No one was happy with the security aspects of the 5 May Agreements; the issue then and subsequently was whether arrangements that would have done more to avert later violence were achievable. The Indonesian position was clear: Indonesia must remain responsible for security during the consultation, and even—in the event of a vote for independence—until after the MPR had made its decision. Some have argued that the governments with the greatest influence in Jakarta could and should have insisted on an international peacekeeping force. A meeting between senior U.S. and Australian officials in late February has been reported as indicating a difference between an Australian desire to avoid a military option and a U.S. conviction that a full-scale peacekeeping operation would be an unavoidable aspect of the transition.[25] But the latter view, which was to prove correct, was a personal one expressed by Assistant Secretary of State Stanley Roth; it certainly did not indicate a willingness of the U.S. government to press Jakarta to accept peacekeepers during a ballot that had yet to be agreed on. During the crucial last week of April, both the Australian and U.S. governments urged Marker not to endanger the agreements by taking too strong a position on the security provisions.[26]

It is doubtful whether any amount of pressure could have induced Habibie and Wiranto to accept international peacekeepers at this juncture. Habibie was already on the defensive; the announcement of the second option had been strongly criticized in Jakarta, including by Habibie's likely rival for the presidency, Megawati Sukarnoputri, and by retired and serving generals. Alatas had indignantly rejected the suggestion of a UN presence for security purposes at the tripartite meeting in March. When the possibility of international peacekeepers was put to Habibie by Howard in their Bali meeting, it was instantly rebuffed and the discussion passed to the numbers of CIVPOL advisers.

There remains the question of whether a firmer stand in the negotiations by the UN and Portugal, backed by the United States and Australia, could have strengthened the security provisions. If so, it could probably only have been in the direction of the more explicit commitments that the UN was proposing, notably to disarm the militia. The inclusion of such commitments in the agreements, instead of in the Secretary-General's memorandum, would have done little to increase the likelihood of their being respected on the ground in East Timor. The UN would still have faced the dilemma that lay ahead: whether to proceed or not to proceed in security conditions that clearly breached Indonesia's commitments under the agreements.

On 5 May, Foreign Ministers Alatas of Indonesia and Jaime Gama of Portugal returned to New York with the full authority of their governments to sign the agreements. The main agreement between the two governments, witnessed by Secretary-General Kofi Annan, had appended to it the constitutional framework for a special autonomy for East Timor. The UN was a full party to the two further agreements: on the modalities for the popular consultation and on security.[27] The date for the ballot was set for Sunday 8 August. The Secretary-General was requested to establish, immediately after the signing, "an appropriate United Nations mission in East Timor to enable him to effectively carry out the popular consultation."

NOTES

1. For a recent account of the positions of successive Australian governments on Indonesia's incorporation of East Timor and the close relationship to Timor Gap negotiations, see Commonwealth of Australia, Senate Foreign Affairs, Defense and Trade References Committee, *Final Report on the Inquiry into East Timor,* 7 December 2000, pp. 151–171. Available online at http://www.aph.gov.au/senate/committee/fadt_ctte/East%20Timor.

2. For a detailed account of the Australian policy review, see Don Greenlees and Robert Garran, *East Timor* (Crows Nest, NSW: Allen and Unwin, forthcoming), chap. 4.

3. The letter is quoted in full and its context described by Tim Fischer, deputy prime minister of Australia at the time it was written, in his *Seven Days in East Timor* (St. Leonards, NSW: Allen and Unwin, 2000), pp. 9–18. See also Alexander Downer, "East Timor—Looking Back on 1999," *Australian Journal of International Affairs* 54, no. 1 (2000).

4. Dewi Fortuna Anwar, former presidential adviser, interviewed in "The Ties That Bind," Australian Broadcasting Corporation, TV broadcast, 14 February 2000. Available online at http://www.abc.net.au/4corners/stories/s99352.htm.

5. For a more detailed account of the discussions within the Indonesian government, see Greenlees and Garran, *East Timor,* chap. 4.

6. Interview with the Portuguese newspaper *Diario de Noticias,* 10 July 1998, in Sarah Niner, ed., *To Resist Is to Win: The Autobiography of Xanana Gusmão* (Richmond, Australia: Aurora Books, 2000), p. 220.

7. Niner, *To Resist Is to Win,* pp. 224–235.

8. See Arnold S. Kohen, *From the Place of the Dead: The Epic Struggles of Bishop Belo of East Timor* (New York: St. Martin's Press, 1999). The letter to Pérez de Cuéllar is at p. 137.

9. Press briefing on East Timor, United Nations, New York, 9 February 1999.

10. *Jakarta Post,* "Ali Alatas Looks Back on 11 Years of Indonesia's Foreign Policy," 2 November 1999.

11. See, for example, Amnesty International, "East Timor: Paramilitary Attacks Jeopardize East Timor's Future," London, 16 April 1999; and "East Timor: Seize the Moment," London, 21 June 1999. For two local accounts of the development and activity of the militia during the period before the arrival of UNAMET, see Helene van Klinken, "Taking the Risk, Paying the Price: East Timorese Vote in Ermera District," and Peter Bartu, "The Militia, the Military and the People of Bobonaro District," in Damien Kingsbury, ed., *Guns and Ballot Boxes: East Timor's Vote for Independence* (Clayton, Australia: Monash Asia Institute, 2000).

12. For example, CNRT leaders in Bobonaro district were forced to take

refuge in the police station and then publicly to "dissolve the CNRT." Peter Bartu, in Kingsbury, ed., *Guns and Ballot Boxes*, pp. 90–91.

13. The Indonesian armed forces were known as Angkatan Bersenjata Republik Indonesia (ABRI; Armed Forces of the Republic of Indonesia) until the separation of the police in April 1999, when they were renamed Tentara Nasional Indonesia (TNI; Indonesian National Military).

14. Komnas HAM, *Report on the Investigation of Human Rights Violations in East Timor, Executive Summary*, Jakarta, 31 January 2000. For a detailed account of the massacre, see Greenlees and Garran, *East Timor*, chap. 5.

15. Amnesty International, *East Timor: Seize the Moment*, p. 20, citing *Agence France Press*, 17 April 1999.

16. Komnas HAM, *Report*, gives fifteen as the number killed. The more detailed account in Amnesty International, *East Timor*, cites the Indonesian authorities' acknowledgment of twelve dead and says the real figure may have been higher.

17. Statement to Seanad Eireann by David Andrews, T.D., minister for foreign affairs, 22 April 1999.

18. The debate within the Indonesian government is described in detail in Greenlees and Garran, *East Timor*, chap. 5.

19. A study group of East Timorese and Indonesian prodemocracy activists in Jakarta concluded that while the authority of the central government of Indonesia appears very limited, "after we peruse and analyze the document we can see that the power of the Central Government is like an octopus roaming all over the sectors of the East Timorese life."

20. *Lusa*, 3 April 1999.

21. See note 13.

22. Press statement, "Falintil Resumes Their Mission in Defense of the People of East Timor," Jakarta, 5 April 1999.

23. *Washington Post*, "E. Timor Failure Puts UN on Spot," 26 September 1999.

24. The Bali meeting is described in Greenlees and Garran, *East Timor*, chap. 5.

25. *The Bulletin*, "The Secret Timor Dossier," Sydney, 12 October 1999.

26. Jamsheed Marker, *Quiet Diplomacy: A Personal Memoire of the East Timor Negotiations* (forthcoming), chap. 14.

27. The full text of the agreements is in *Report of the Secretary-General*, A/53/951-S/1999/513, 5 May 1999, and reprinted in Appendix 3. It consists of Annex I: Agreement Between the Republic of Indonesia and the Portuguese Republic on the Question of East Timor (the main agreement), to which is appended A Constitutional Framework for a Special Autonomy for East Timor (the autonomy proposal); Annex II: Agreement Regarding the Modalities for the Popular Consultation of the East Timorese Through a Direct Ballot (the modalities agreement); and Annex III: East Timor Popular Consultation (the security agreement).

3

Launching UNAMET

THE PLAN AND MANDATE

In presenting the agreements to the Security Council on 5 May 1999, the Secretary-General referred to the logistical problems the UN would face in carrying out the consultation in such a short timeframe. He announced the opening of a trust fund for voluntary contributions, which would enable him to proceed with establishing a UN presence in East Timor as soon as possible, without waiting for the assessed budgetary process. He undertook to report on the logistical and personnel requirements once they had been identified.[1] On 7 May, the Security Council welcomed the agreements, noted the Secretary-General's concerns regarding the security situation, and expressed its intention to make a prompt decision on establishing a UN mission as soon as he reported on its proposed mandate, size, structure, and budget.[2]

Those with operational responsibility were dismayed by the seemingly unrealistic timetable the negotiators had agreed to. The UN system moved, as it now had to, with unusual speed. The day before the signing of the agreements, a further assessment mission was on its way to East Timor to update the Secretariat's evaluation of the political and security situation, identify facilities for the mission, and obtain information for a detailed operational plan. A small advance team, including political officers and the spokesperson as well as logistical staff, established the UN presence in Dili, even before the formal mandating of the mission. On 22 May, the Secretary-General was able to present his proposals for the UN Mission in East Timor (UNAMET);[3] he had informed the Security Council the previous day of my appointment as his Special Representative (SRSG) for the East Timor Popular Consultation. As detailed in the subsequent budget submission, these proposals envis-

aged a political component of 15 officers; an electoral team at headquarters and in 8 regional offices comprising 28 professionals, with 400
UN Volunteers (UNVs) as district electoral officers; 9 public information officers; 275 police; and 271 administrative and support staff,
including 16 security officers. The total UNV contingent was planned
as 425, including medical personnel and a support unit; it would rise to
500 as the requirements of the ballot exceeded expectations. It was estimated that the mission would need some 4,000 local staff, reaching a
peak at the time of the poll. Three eminent international experts would
be appointed to serve as an independent Electoral Commission based in
Dili, while polling outside East Timor would be conducted by the
Australian Electoral Commission and the International Organization for
Migration. UNAMET would have an office in Jakarta; headed by a senior political officer, this office would maintain liaison with the
Indonesian authorities and with Xanana Gusmão as long as he remained
in detention there. Human rights would be integrated into different
aspects of the mission's components, and the Office of the High
Commissioner for Human Rights nominated two officers who served in
the political and electoral components. The Office for the Coordination
of Humanitarian Affairs (OCHA) nominated a humanitarian affairs
officer.

The nature of the UN presence to implement the ballot had initially
been conceived by the Department of Political Affairs (DPA), which
had been responsible for supporting Marker throughout the negotiations. As operational planning was under way, it became clear that the
mission would include police, and the Department of Peacekeeping
Operations (DPKO) became involved. DPKO participated in the second
assessment mission and, in the light of its somber report on the security
situation it encountered in East Timor, strongly urged the inclusion of
military officers within UNAMET. There was no internal disagreement
about the desirability of this, since it was well understood that the TNI
(or at least significant elements within it) were giving active support to
the militia and that the police could not go against the military to
attempt to curb them. Influencing the TNI and holding them as well as
the police accountable for any failure to ensure security was therefore
crucial, and military officers would stand a better chance of doing this.
However, the negotiators were concerned that Indonesia might react
strongly against a proposal that had not been envisaged in the agreements. The intention was signaled in the Secretary-General's 22 May
report, but no figure was stated pending the outcome of consultations
with the Indonesians. A contingent of eighty was proposed to them,
although some in DPKO argued for a higher number. Wiranto quite

readily gave his assent to a maximum of fifty. To satisfy the Indonesians as to the limitations of their role, they were called military liaison officers (MLOs) rather than the more usual military observers. Their inclusion brought the total international staffing of UNAMET to a little over 1,000.

While it was clear that neither the CIVPOL nor the MLOs were to have enforcement authority of any kind, the question of whether they should carry sidearms for self-defense preoccupied some contributing governments, especially Australia and the United States. Within the Australian government, the issue became a matter of cabinet discussion. The UN Secretariat opposed the carrying of weapons, as did I and UNAMET's Australian police commissioner, Alan Mills, whose view finally helped to sway Canberra. The carrying of arms, we argued, might incorrectly give rise to the expectation that CIVPOL had a responsibility for providing security and would encourage the use of weapons against them. A pistol would in any case be no match if an officer were faced by a well-armed individual or an angry mob.

The U.S. requirement to consult Congress meant that UNAMET could not be formally mandated by the Security Council, triggering budgetary authorization, until 11 June.[4] Yet the timetable implied the opening of voter registration by 22 June.

ESTABLISHING UNAMET

A number of factors made it possible for UNAMET to be established with a speed that was unprecedented—and that could not be expected to be repeated in the absence of those factors. The use of a trust fund that received immediate voluntary contributions meant that financial commitments did not have to await the authorization of assessed contributions. The largest contributions were made by Australia, Portugal, Japan, and the United States, followed by the European Union; ultimately, of UNAMET's total eventual cost of around $80 million, about $50 million was met by voluntary contributions, in cash and kind. In-kind contributions from nearby Australia overcame some potential procurement bottlenecks and included UNAMET's first vehicles and the helicopters used throughout the popular consultation. The UN's Logistics Base at Brindisi, Italy, had a substantial amount of equipment immediately available; UNAMET was fortunate in being at the head of the surge of missions in 1999 that would rapidly deplete it. Asia's economic collapse was UNAMET's good fortune; stocks of vehicles were available to be flown to East Timor from Tokyo. But no good fortune should detract from the sense of urgency in the Secretariat and the extraordinary efforts of the first administrative and logistical staff sent out to establish the mission.

I arrived in Dili on 1 June, after meetings in Jakarta en route. The spokesperson and head of public information, David Wimhurst (Canada), was already in post. The senior team assembled gradually: Police Commissioner Alan Mills (Australia), Chief Electoral Officer Jeff Fischer (United States), Chief Military Liaison Officer Brigadier Rezaqul Haider (Bangladesh), Chief Political Officer Beng Yong Chew (Singapore), and Chief Administrative Officer Johannes Wortel (Netherlands). UNAMET's Jakarta office was headed by Tamrat Samuel (Eritrea).

The quality of staffing of the mission was exceptionally high; UNAMET benefited again from being the first of the major missions launched in 1999 and from being understood to face an extremely difficult task and tight timetable. Thus, electoral and public information staff with proven records from other missions were rapidly gathered together. Equally important was the inclusion in the small political affairs team of political officers with particular knowledge of Indonesia and East Timor, and appropriate language skills, from outside the UN system, as well as key members of the DPA team.

DPA retained lead responsibility for UNAMET, and as head of the mission I reported to the Secretary-General through the Under-Secretary-General for Political Affairs, Kieran Prendergast. Prompt and effective political support and general backstopping was provided by DPA's Asia and the Pacific Division, headed by Francesc Vendrell, whose small East Timor team was slightly expanded for this purpose. DPA's Electoral Assistance Division continued to give close support to the Chief Electoral Officer—support that included visits from its director, Carina Perelli. The Department of Public Information had conceived, and supported, the public information team. As with other major field missions, administrative and logistical support was provided by the Field Administration and Logistics Division within DPKO, while DPKO recruited and supported the CIVPOL and MLO contingents. A DPA-led task force coordinated the interdepartmental effort to support UNAMET.

The local authorities had identified and made available excellent premises—a former teacher training college—for UNAMET's headquarters. The raising of the UN flag there for the first time on 4 June embroiled UNAMET in immediate controversy, despite our care to ensure the presence of representatives of the Indonesian and Portuguese governments and both pro-autonomy and pro-independence leaders. It was an emotional day for the East Timorese; the raising of the UN flag emboldened the pro-independence groups and worried the pro-integrationists. A leading CNRT underground organizer, David Ximenes, who had been in hiding for months, appeared at the ceremony and helped to calm a wildly enthusiastic pro-independence crowd outside the compound, many of them from the neighboring University of East Timor. This was not enough to prevent a few of them from attacking and damaging the cars of the governor, the mayor of Dili, and a pro-autonomy leader as they left the event.

The engagement of local staff was a matter of early contention that would eventually have lethal consequences. UNAMET was accused of favoring independence supporters in its recruitment. There was certainly no conscious bias, but in addition to the fact that there was a pro-independence majority in the population as a whole, as the consultation would show, two other factors were in operation. UNAMET desperately needed English speakers, and these were mostly found among recent university students who were even more overwhelmingly pro-independence in their sympathies than the general population; educated supporters of integration were more likely to be already employed in local government. Moreover, it was those who had wanted a referendum who came forward enthusiastically to join in the work of UNAMET; those who had never favored and felt threatened by it were likely to hang back. When a pro-autonomy party put forward candidates for recruitment and UNAMET expressed willingness to interview them, they never appeared. Whatever the personal opinions of local staff, it was stressed that they must act in accordance with UNAMET's neutrality, and they were required to sign an undertaking to that effect. With the rarest of exceptions, it was a commitment that they respected.

The first electoral and administrative staff were rapidly out traveling in the regions to identify space for regional offices and registration centers. Local authorities were mostly very cooperative in identifying the limited options, but living conditions for those working in some regional and subregional offices were going to be extremely basic. Predeployment training for the district electoral officers (DEOs), CIVPOL, and MLOs commenced as the first groups arrived in Darwin in Australia's Northern Territory, one hour and forty minutes flying time from Dili in the veteran Hercules C-130 leased by UNAMET. Absence of accommodation as well as speed dictated that the majority of them were deployed to the regions the day they were flown to the island.

The largest recruitment effort was that of the UN Volunteer

program in the immediate deployment of 400 DEOs. The selection proved an excellent one: coming from more than seventy countries, many of them had previous UN electoral experience and had lived in tough conditions. The first group arrived in Darwin in mid-June, and the last had been trained and deployed to East Timor by 8 July. Only in Cambodia had a larger contingent of UNVs been recruited, and nowhere with such speed. The other contingent whose presence would be most far-flung and vital to local confidence, the CIVPOL, could not be assembled until after the Security Council had conferred the formal mandate on 11 June; their deployment was complete on 10 July. The CIVPOL were drawn from twenty-seven countries[5] and the MLOs from thirteen.[6] Despite extraordinary efforts, it became clear that DEOs, CIVPOL, and vehicles could not all be fielded in time for registration to open on 22 June, the latest date consistent with a ballot on 8 August.

Indonesia sent its own additional representatives to East Timor. On 11 May, a special ministerial task force had been established in Jakarta, headed by the coordinating minister for political and security affairs, and comprising the minister for foreign affairs, minister for home affairs, minister for defense/chief of the armed forces, minister for justice, chief of the national police, and head of the national intelligence coordinating agency. The task force was represented in Dili by the Indonesian Task Force for the Implementation of the Popular Consultation in East Timor.

The East Timor task force was headed by a former permanent representative to the UN in Geneva, Ambassador Agus Tarmidzi, and comprised representatives of the ministries and bodies forming the national task force. These included two TNI generals, the senior being Major-General Zacky Anwar Makarim, who until January 1999 had been head of military intelligence. Junior members of the Indonesian Task Force, mostly foreign service officers, were posted in the districts. Indonesian police officers who had served with the UN and spoke English were deployed to act as liaison officers with the CIVPOL, and once it was agreed that UNAMET would have its contingent of MLOs, a similar group of military liaison officers was dispatched—arriving before most of the MLOs themselves.

The agreements provided for Portugal and Indonesia to send official observer delegations to East Timor, and they eventually agreed that each delegation would be fifty-strong. In the case of Indonesia, this only added to the strong official presence headed by the Indonesian Task Force, but for Portugal this provided its most substantial presence in the territory since its 1975 withdrawal and an important source of information as the popular consultation proceeded.

FIRST FINDINGS

As UNAMET's first political officers arrived to join the advance team, they began to travel out of Dili. They encountered a pro-autonomy campaign in full swing and came to understand the extent of the grip the militia had established and the consequences of the violence of recent months.

A pro-autonomy party, Forum Persatuan, Demokrasi dan Keadilan (FPDK; Forum for Unity, Democracy and Justice), had declared its existence on 27 January. Its leading figures were mostly local government officers, headed by the *bupati* of Dili, Domingos Soares.[7] The links between the local administration, the FPDK, the militia, and the TNI were so close that they constituted a single operation to counter pro-independence activities and ensure a pro-autonomy vote. Documentary evidence emerged to confirm the obvious suspicion that the FPDK and the militia were heavily funded from government budgets.[8] Subsequently, in April, a second pro-autonomy party, Barisan Rakyat Timor Timur (BRTT; East Timor People's Front), was established under Francisco Lopes da Cruz, a former UDT leader and vice-governor of East Timor, who was serving as a special ambassador in the Indonesian foreign ministry. It too benefited from government funding and close links to the local administration.

Before the arrival of UNAMET, a series of meetings was under way throughout the districts and subdistricts, at which the local population would be required to gather and affirm support for autonomy within Indonesia. Militia and FPDK cadres, local government officials, the TNI, and police would typically all be present. At some meetings, participants would be required to swear oaths, accompanied by blood drinking. UNAMET officials became direct witnesses to such meetings in their early travel to the districts and subdistricts. They encountered pro-autonomy banners displayed across highways and the red-and-white Indonesian flag flying outside every individual dwelling in many towns and villages, in what their occupants said was a means of self-protection against the militia. In some places, the charred remains of dwellings bore witness to the consequences of failing to display the correct allegiance. Civil servants were told that they had to support autonomy and were required to sign statements pledging their support or leave their jobs. In some cases, they were dismissed or suspended and their salaries withheld.

This coercive pro-autonomy campaign had begun well before the 5 May Agreements but continued long after the signing of the agreements rendered it inadmissible. The agreements specified a designated period, after registration, for a peaceful and democratic political campaign, governed by a code of conduct to be proposed by UNAMET, in which the two sides would have equal opportunity to disseminate their views. They excluded officials of the governments of Indonesia and Portugal from participating in the campaign and required the "absolute neutrality" of the TNI and police. East Timorese government officials might campaign in their personal capacity only: "All such campaigning will be carried out strictly according to the Code of Conduct without use of public funds and government resources or recourse to pressure of office."

By mid-June, UNAMET had gathered a dossier of evidence of these breaches of the agreements and submitted it to the Indonesian Task Force; it supplemented it in July. Initially, Indonesian officials defended the legitimacy of activities to "socialize" the autonomy proposal, although even if they had been purely informative in character, this was a responsibility given to the UN alone under the agreements. But the budgets earmarked funds for local militia, the FPDK, and the BRTT, as well as for campaign activities of government officials and the military. They made provision for the distribution of food and other benefits as part of the socialization campaign and for *adat* (traditional) activities, such as the blood-drinking ceremonies UNAMET had witnessed. A letter from the governor of East Timor, Abilio José Osorio Soares, prescribed the action to be taken against civil servants disloyal to Indonesia, including suspension and dismissal. This was reflected in letters from lower-level officials. UNAMET urged that the requirements of the agreements be circulated, together with firm instructions that they must be strictly observed and must prevail over any previous instructions. Only in late July was UNAMET informed that some appropriate action was being taken.

UNAMET also quickly became direct witness to the operation of the militia. A UNAMET team, ironically engaged on a successful mission to bring back a policeman and a militia member held by Falintil, encountered three groups of militia, together with TNI soldiers under whose direction they appeared to be operating. They saw them forcing inhabitants to leave their village against their will, burning personal property, and assaulting an old man. Two days later, I was being accompanied by a military member of the Indonesian Task Force and journalists when I stopped to question a group of militia being drilled by the roadside. The former military officer training them denied that they had weapons, but local people offered information that led the CIVPOL officer accompanying me to uncover their cache of homemade firearms. These were minor examples of what had become commonplace, but they enabled UNAMET to speak on the basis of firsthand experience as well as the accumulation of testimony.

Most serious of all was the confirmation of the consequences of the months of militia violence: the tens of thousands of internally displaced persons (IDPs). They told of attacks on pro-independence communities in which some had been killed, the rape of women (who in some cases were subjected to continuing sexual slavery), and the destruction of many homes and whole villages. Estimating the numbers of IDPs was difficult; they were scattered, mostly in small groups, in towns, villages, the hills, and church compounds, although there were two large concentrations of at least 3,000 each near the boundary between Ermera and Liquiça districts. Their existence was officially denied, and access to them by humanitarian agencies had been prevented, by threats against international as well as local personnel. The militia grip had become so pervasive that most of them remained subject to it. But the investigations of UNAMET's humanitarian affairs officer and the representative of the UN High Commissioner for Refugees (UNHCR) soon suggested that the local NGOs' estimate of 40,000 in June was not exaggerated. The IDPs, lacking access to adequate supplies of food and medicines, presented a major humanitarian issue. But the nature of the phenomenon was political: they were the victims of a campaign of intimidation to coerce a vote against independence, which remained the motive for their continued subjection to militia control. Ensuring that this large section of the population was not disfranchised by the action the TNI and militia had taken against them became a major preoccupation for UNAMET.

It was thus clear in mid-June that the security conditions deemed necessary for the consultation had not begun to exist. The presence of UNAMET, international journalists, and others was leading to a growing normality of life in Dili, with its citizens again feeling able to move after darkness; the impact of the international presence, especially the CIVPOL, in the districts was yet to be tested.

POSTPONING REGISTRATION

The possibility of opening registration on 22 June was thus precluded both by the security situation and by UNAMET's personnel and logistical limitations. A three-week postponement was put to Indonesia and Portugal. The latter, although eager to avoid slippage in the timetable, accepted the inevitable. President Habibie too was willing to concur when he received Marker and me in Jakarta, but on two conditions. He insisted that the delay should be attributed solely to the UN's being unready, and not to the security situation. The second issue was a new one—the date inscribed in the agreements for the ballot, 8 August, fell on a Sunday. Indonesia now insisted that a Sunday was inappropriate, citing the religious sensibilities of the predominantly Christian East Timorese. Portugal, assuming that the real motive was a realization that a Sunday poll might enhance the influence of the church, resisted a change. East Timor's bishops, consulted by the UN, were more amused than prescriptive; they did not share the Indonesian view that Christian sensibilities were at stake, but neither did they believe that the influence of the church in encouraging the faithful to vote according to their consciences was limited to Sundays. The issue lingered on in tripartite discussions, and it was weeks later that a Monday was agreed upon.

On 22 June, the Secretary-General reported again to the Security Council.[9] He noted that "in many areas, pro-integration militias, believed by many observers to be operating with the acquiescence of elements of the army, carry out acts of violence against the population and exert an intimidating influence over it." He based a postponement on both the security and the logistical constraints, stating:

> I would be unable to certify that the necessary conditions exist to begin the operational phases of the consultation process, given the security situation and the absence of a level playing field. I would also wish to allow UNAMET sufficient time to reach the strength necessary to begin registration successfully. . . . It is therefore my intention that UNAMET not begin the operational phases until it is fully deployed, which would also give the Indonesian authorities time to address the pending security concerns.

The Secretary-General's determination regarding security would be postponed for three weeks, with registration then to open on 13 July; there would be a two-week postponement of the ballot date.

By now, I and my senior police and military colleagues were in almost daily discussion of incidents and indicators of the security situation with the Indonesians, especially with the Indonesian Task Force's security adviser, General Zacky. UNAMET's initial inquiries about evidence of militia in training had been met with an explanation of the legitimacy of *wanra* and *kamra,* official auxiliaries to the army and police respectively; but these existed separately from the militia, although perhaps with some overlapping membership. Next the militia were represented as Pam Swakarsa: government-funded community self-defense groups, formed under this name in different parts of Indonesia. Eurico Guterres, the commander of the Dili-based Aitarak militia, was appointed by the *bupati* of Dili to head Pam Swakarsa in that city. UNAMET was told on some occasions that the existence of Pam Swakarsa in East Timor was justified by the fact that Falintil remained under arms, and on other occasions that giving the militia the status of Pam Swakarsa was a means of bringing them under official control. We accepted neither argument and protested that the agreements required the police to be solely responsible for law and order.

The limitations of the police in preventing or responding to militia violence were seen when UNAMET itself became its target. On the day of its opening, 29 June, the regional office in Maliana, Bobonaro district, was heavily stoned by militia, with injuries to local people and a light injury to a woman DEO. This district bordering West Timor was the one whose authorities were from beginning to end the most flagrantly hostile to the popular consultation.[10] The Indonesian Task Force regretted the incident but portrayed it as the by-product of a "brawl" between pro-autonomy and pro-independence supporters, with the UNAMET office becoming an unintended target when the latter sought refuge there. UNAMET's own information indicated that local divisions began when a militia attack on the UNAMET office was being planned, under the direction of the TNI district commander and the local head of military intelligence. The police response was slow and inadequate in the extreme. Shaken electoral staff were temporarily withdrawn to Dili. The next day they were joined there by electoral staff withdrawn from the eastern-district town of Viqueque, where a staff residence had been surrounded by armed militia shouting death threats. UNAMET staff in Liquiça experienced a series of threats from militia roaming through the town with weapons. Then, on 4 July, militia attacked a humanitarian convoy passing through Liquiça town; local NGO workers were brutally beaten and injured, and UNAMET's humanitarian affairs officer was directly targeted. As staff were being evacuated from the town, UNAMET's helicopter and vehicles were attacked by armed militia.[11]

At the same time, UNAMET was being subjected to a hostile media campaign, with statements issued in the name of the FPDK rapidly being given official Indonesian circulation through the spokesperson for the Indonesian Task Force in Dili and by the Indonesian Permanent Mission in New York. The campaign extended to deliberate fabrication. An Australian CIVPOL officer was falsely accused of "ransacking" a house when inspecting it, together with Indonesian police, after allegations of illegal storage of arms. UNAMET received reliable information that two days after the event it was indeed ransacked—by TNI soldiers—and then filmed by Indonesian television. The existence of a contemporary video made at the house by a foreign journalist, showing the presence of Indonesian police and the occupants' smiling consent to the brief inspection, averted the showing of the fabricated "evidence" of UNAMET's impropriety, but the public allegations were never corrected. During the Liquiça attack, a homemade gun was dropped in the vehicle of UNAMET's humanitarian affairs officer, and it was publicly alleged that there had been Falintil people in the vehicle and shots fired from it; the officer became the only person charged with unlawful possession of a weapon in a territory where firearms were brandished daily. UNAMET's spokesperson, whose forthright statements had from the outset been objected to, was the subject of serious death threats as well as public criticism. The Indonesian journalists in East Timor, for whom UNAMET organized daily briefings in their own language, increasingly expressed private dismay at what they witnessed, but they were also frank about the limits on their freedom to report fully. Most of what appeared in the Jakarta press, especially from the official news agency, Antara, faithfully reflected the misinformation campaign.

The stoning of the Maliana office and the attack on the humanitarian convoy were captured on film by foreign television crews and made dramatic footage on worldwide news bulletins. The Secretary-General and the Security Council issued strongly worded statements, first in response to the Maliana incident and again after the Liquiça attack. I flew to Jakarta to put UNAMET's information regarding militia activity and TNI involvement direct to Wiranto, who announced the dispatch of additional police to East Timor. Electoral preparations were temporarily suspended. The Indonesian government and the Security Council were told that the current security situation could not be judged adequate for the opening of registration. Governments made strong bilateral representations; perhaps the most significant of these was the visit to Jakarta of Australia's vice chief of defense staff in late June to deliver a strong message to the TNI based on Australia's intelligence on the TNI-militia relationship.[12] With the date looming for the UN's postponed determination of the security conditions, Habibie instructed members of his ministerial task force, including Feisal Tanjung, Alatas, Wiranto, and the head of the police, to go to Dili on 12 July. While the official Indonesian position was to press the UN to maintain the timetable for an expedited registration and vote, what was happening on the ground was clearly an effort to subvert that process. It was hard to know which was the real policy of the Indonesian government.

With registration due to open on 13 July, a critical moment in the UN's decisionmaking had arrived. With the support of the chief electoral officer (CEO) and the police commissioner, I initially recommended that electoral preparations should remain suspended until the

Indonesian government had taken action resulting in clear improvement in the security situation, while UNAMET should maintain the logistical readiness to open registration as soon as this had occurred. International publicity had focused on the intimidation of UNAMET staff, but the greater concern was security for the participation of East Timorese voters. The security requirements set out by the Secretary-General at the time of the agreements were nowhere near being fulfilled. In the light of its experience, UNAMET drew up a further set of criteria. The responsibilities of the Indonesian police must include prompt arrest and prosecution of those involved in violence, including attacks against UNAMET, and rapid and adequate intervention to stop violent attacks. The control of armed groups should include the arrest of those carrying weapons, an end to the incorporation of militia into Pam Swakarsa units, and the closing down of militia roadblocks. IDPs must be able to return home and the CNRT to operate openly. Members of the TNI most obviously involved with militia must be reassigned away, and the TNI and police must stop campaigning. These criteria were conveyed to the Indonesian Task Force in Dili and discussed in detail with the task force and with the East Timor TNI and police commanders.

Although there was sympathy in New York for my recommendation of a postponement, Marker was keenly aware of the Indonesian insistence that the ballot must take place no later than the end of August. After a good deal of agonizing among his advisers, the Secretary-General wrote on 10 July to inform the Security Council that, in order to allow for concrete steps to follow the visit of the Indonesian authorities to Dili on 12 July, he proposed to start registration on 16 July—the last date consistent with a ballot before the end of August. But the decision to go ahead had not yet been made. "The requisite certification of security conditions and the opening of registration would be confirmed if concrete progress is made on improving the security situation in East Timor as defined in the criteria."[13]

In reality, for registration to open on 16 July, the final decision to go ahead had to be made no later than 14 July, which hardly allowed the effects of the pressures and the ministerial visit to Dili to be assessed. But the security situation had calmed down; the pressure had induced arrests in connection with the Maliana and Liquiça attacks, the Liquiça police chief had been replaced, and UNAMET had been able to engage the Indonesians in the most detailed discussions and commitments so far achieved. I conveyed to New York my preference for a further postponement of the opening of registration to allow a proper assessment of whether the latest commitments, unlike those made previously, would be reflected in real improvement on the ground. But if the importance of not allowing the ballot to slip beyond the end of August was judged to be overriding, I said we were ready to go ahead and open registration on 16 July—on the basis that this did not constitute a positive assessment of the security conditions and that registration would be suspended if the security situation had not improved substantially by its midpoint.

The stakes were high. To proceed with the consultation in the midst of violence could not only put the East Timorese and the UN's own staff at risk but also set the scene for the UN to sanction an outcome that was the result of intimidation. Yet to suspend the process risked handing victory to those who were bent on preventing the vote from taking place and losing what many East Timorese, including Gusmão, believed might prove the unique window of opportunity for them to determine their own future. On 14 July, the Secretary-General wrote again to the Security Council. He was unable to conclude that the necessary security conditions, called for by the agreements, existed; violence and intimidation continued to be carried out with impunity by pro-autonomy militias. But he had decided to begin the registration, "based on positive assurances by the Indonesian authorities, on the condition that meaningful, visible improvements in the security situation will be observed in the immediate future." There would be another assessment by UNAMET halfway through the registration period.[14]

NOTES

1. *Report of the Secretary-General,* A/53/951-S/1999/513, 5 May 1999.

2. *Security Council Resolution 1236 (1999),* 7 May 1999.

3. *Report of the Secretary-General,* S/1999/595, 22 May 1999.

4. *Security Council Resolution 1246 (1999),* 11 June 1999, reprinted in Appendix 4.

5. Argentina, Australia, Austria, Bangladesh, Brazil, Canada, Egypt, Ghana, Ireland, Japan, Jordan, Malaysia, Mozambique, Nepal, New Zealand, Pakistan, the Philippines, the Republic of Korea, the Russian Federation, Senegal, Spain, Sweden, Thailand, the United Kingdom, the United States, Uruguay, and Zimbabwe.

6. Australia, Austria, Bangladesh, Brazil, Denmark, Ireland, Malaysia, New Zealand, the Russian Federation, Thailand, the United Kingdom, the United States, and Uruguay.

7. East Timor was divided into thirteen *kabupaten* (regencies or districts), including Dili, each under the administration of a *bupati.*

8. Evidence continued to emerge once East Timor was under international administration; see "Dateline," SBS TV broadcast, 16 February 2000. Available online at http://203.15.102.140/dateline/test/transcript.php3?date=

2000-02-16&title=Timor+Terror+Fund. See also Don Greenlees and Robert Garran, *East Timor* (Crows Nest, NSW: Allen and Unwin, forthcoming), chap. 6.

9. *Report of the Secretary-General,* S/1999/705, 22 June 1999.

10. See Peter Bartu, "The Militia, the Military and the People of Bobonaro District," in Damien Kingsbury, ed., *Guns and Ballot Boxes: East Timor's Vote for Independence* (Clayton, Australia: Monash Asia Institute, 2000), pp. 81–98.

11. The Indonesian government's accounts of the Maliana and Liquiça incidents were set out in a letter from Foreign Minister Alatas, circulated in Letter Dated 12 July 1999 from the Permanent Representative of Indonesia Addressed to the President of the Security Council, S/1999/782, 13 July 1999.

12. Described in Greenlees and Garran, *East Timor,* chap. 8.

13. Letter dated 10 July 1999 from the Secretary-General addressed to the President of the Security Council, S/1999/773.

14. Letter dated 14 July 1999 from the Secretary-General addressed to the President of the Security Council, S/1999/788.

4

Preparing the Ballot

THE GROUNDWORK FOR REGISTRATION

Confirmation that registration of voters for the popular consultation would begin at 7 A.M. on 16 July was given to the DEOs throughout East Timor on the morning of 15 July. Although the DEOs had been fully deployed and the registration kits distributed, the decision to proceed came to the field as something of a surprise—many thought the level of violence was too intense for the process to go forward. Dili headquarters itself was far from certain that it would prove possible to open all 200 registration centers—still less that the registration period could be completed successfully, with the tens of thousands of IDPs able to register within the twenty days allotted.

Now, for the first time, the factor that would determine the success of the popular consultation made itself clear: the determination of the people of East Timor to have their say regarding their future and their courage in defying violence to do so. Almost as soon as registration opened, the queues began to form. All but six of the 200 centers were able to open on 16 July: two for logistical reasons and four because of security. These opened the next day, and at the end of the first five days, over 100,000 people had already registered.

This was evidence too of the success of the well-considered plans formulated by the Electoral Assistance Division (EAD) at UN headquarters and developed by UNAMET's electoral component, as well as of the intense public information campaign. Only for the third time was the UN actually conducting a ballot rather than assisting or monitoring one; the experience of the UN-organized Cambodian elections of 1993 informed the planning.[1] The Indonesian general election had been held on 7 June, including in East Timor, and gave some indication of requirements there. But the eligibility criteria for the popular consultation, set out in the agreements, were unique, based on neither citizenship nor residence. To register to vote, a person had to be over seventeen years of age, be born in East Timor or have at least one parent born in East Timor, or be married to someone in one of the latter two categories. About 400,000 people had registered in East Timor for the Indonesian election, and it was estimated that about 20 percent of these were non-Timorese ineligible under the criteria. Thus, the voter population for the popular consultation was initially estimated to be between 350,000 and 400,000. Later it became clear that many East Timorese had not registered for the Indonesian election, and planning was done on a higher figure.[2]

As soon as the agreements had been signed, EAD in New York, together with representatives of the Australian Electoral Commission and senior electoral personnel selected for UNAMET, began drafting the detailed formal instructions, the Electoral Directions, eventually issued under my authority as SRSG on 18 June. The UNVs arriving in Darwin were trained in their functions as DEOs and as trainers of the staff who would be locally recruited. Priority was given to the registration procedures. Other issues would have to be addressed with flexibility as they were raised throughout the process, so the Electoral Directions allowed the CEO to issue modifications in the form of "notifications," drafted by UNAMET's legal officer.

The most difficult issue to be addressed before registration opened was that of the documentation to establish eligibility. Two opposing objectives had to be balanced: substantial protection against the registration of non–East Timorese, and sufficient inclusiveness to afford all qualified East Timorese a reasonable opportunity to participate. Reconciling these objectives was made more difficult by the knowledge that many people, especially those internally displaced, had lost documents or their documents had been deliberately destroyed against their will. The integrity of official Indonesian documentation could not be relied upon. It was decided to require two forms of documentation: one as proof of identity (expected to contain a picture and, most commonly, an Indonesian identity card); the other to establish eligibility (for example, a certificate of birth, baptism, or marriage).

It was recognized, however, that many eligible East Timorese might not have access to the necessary documents and might thus be disfranchised. After much internal debate, UNAMET instituted an affidavit procedure. In the absence of sufficient documentation, an individual could produce an affidavit, attesting to his/her identity and birth in East Timor. This had to be sworn before a religious leader or village chief and witnessed by a registered voter who knew the applicant. The affidavit procedure was controversial, as it was feared that it might open the window for abuse, but without it, many who were genuinely eligible would be excluded.

INFORMING THE VOTERS

Uncertainty about the opening of registration, and the time required to consider the documentary issues and consult knowledgeable East Timorese about them, did not allow for widespread explanation of the procedures. UNAMET's public information team had had to begin by negotiating its access to television, radio, and print media and by translating basic documentation—most notably, the autonomy proposal—so that it was available in all four of the official languages of the consultation process: Tetun, Bahasa Indonesia, Portuguese, and English. After disseminating a message from the Secretary-General and otherwise introducing UNAMET and stressing its neutrality, the information campaign focused on how to participate. It was evident that the voter population was already highly motivated.

The information campaign gave particular emphasis to radio, given the high rate of illiteracy and problems of reaching outlying communities. UNAMET produced two radio programs broadcast daily on state and church-owned radio stations, both for fifteen minutes daily in each of the four languages. UNAMET programming was also rebroadcast on the international service of Portuguese radio. A half-hour daily television program was estimated to reach some 180,000 viewers. The back page of East Timor's only daily newspaper, *Suara Timor Timur*, was the initial outlet for written information, subsequently reprinted as handbills for local distribution.[3] These included serialization of the full text and explanation of the autonomy proposal. UNAMET's particular responsibility in this respect was further fulfilled by the publication and distribution of 50,000 copies in booklet form. Even the radio campaign was limited in its outreach by East Timor's mountainous terrain, but material initially produced for radio became the basis of voter education cassettes, distributed to the DEOs and played on UNAMET's vehicle radios in the villages. Specific bulletins, and illustrated materials to overcome the literacy gap, were produced to explain procedures, beginning with the registration process.[4]

OVERCOMING INTIMIDATION AND DISPLACEMENT

On 19 July, the fourth day of registration and one week after the visit of the Indonesian ministers to Dili, I was able to report to New York that the TNI and the militia seemed more subdued. TNI East Timor commander Suratman provided UNAMET with a series of orders and instructions he had issued that, if followed, would go some way to reflect the UN's requirements on TNI neutrality. The active involvement of the East Timor police chief, Colonel Timbul Silaen—with whom UNAMET's police commissioner had established a cooperative relationship—was proving valuable in addressing particular local problems of intimidation. The incidents that had so far affected registration centers appeared to be more of a localized militia activity than an overall campaign to prevent registration. Nevertheless, the level of threat and intimidation to the local population remained high. This assessment was reflected in the Secretary-General's 20 July report to the Security Council, which noted that militia activities continued to pose a fundamental challenge to a credible consultation process, the security situation remaining particularly serious in the western districts.[5]

Indeed, as UNAMET reported in its mid-July analysis, there had been no change in the fundamentals that lay at the heart of insecurity: no steps had been taken to disband the militia, the TNI was still fully deployed down to village level, and whatever their formal instructions, the TNI and government authorities continued to lend their political, material, and logistical support to the militia and other pro-autonomy forces. The leading human rights NGO in East Timor, Yayasan HAK, established a network of local observers and reported efforts by local officials, the TNI, and militia to obstruct and threaten those registering in accordance with UNAMET's requirements and to mobilize fraudulent voters from West Timor.[6] Some of the first international observer groups had also begun to function: the Carter Center and the International Federation for East Timor both reported on the continued militia intimidation but were encouraged by the high turnout for registration.[7] Militia violence or threats continued to require occasional temporary closures throughout the registration, but immediate troubleshooting, led by UNAMET's police commissioner with good cooperation from his senior Indonesian counterparts, ensured that no center stayed closed for more than a single day. In the end, fewer than twenty out of a total of 4,400 registration center days were lost as a result of security closures.

A substantially illiterate population understood and adapted itself with impressive alacrity to relatively complex registration procedures.[8]

From the outset there were few rejected applications (mostly of the eager underaged), although many who had queued once had to return with further documentation before knowledge of the requirements spread. There was little attempted fraud, despite extensive use of affidavits in some places. The DEOs' assessment that this was the case would be confirmed later when almost no challenges were made to the published list. There were protests at the refusal to allow registration on the basis of the Indonesian identity card alone, and the pro-integration *bupati* of Bobonaro district sought confrontation by instructing his supporters to refuse to present a second document. But this protest only confirmed UNAMET's judgment: the most significant attempt at organized fraud involved an effort in his district to bring people from West Timor and issue them with brand new identity cards.

Any attempted obstruction was of limited effectiveness. UNAMET had decided not to issue daily figures or a regional breakdown, in case this should give rise to further interference. The TNI was clearly attempting to monitor the process, and regional military commander Damiri was quoted in the media as stating that by the fifth day of registration, only 33,633 people had registered (the actual total was more than three times this figure). When the Secretary-General wrote to inform the Security Council at midpoint that registration would continue, he revealed that in the first ten days, 239,893 East Timorese had registered—233,716 of them in East Timor.[9] At this rate, the UN's higher estimates for the voter population would be exceeded.

UNAMET therefore recommended the continuation of registration, but once again it was important that this was not interpreted as a statement that security conditions were now adequate. The Secretary-General told the Security Council that registration was being continued "on the understanding that the Indonesian authorities will work with UNAMET to achieve the further necessary improvements in the security situation and urgently address the problem of internal displacement." The completion of registration and the continuation of the process would depend on these improvements being achieved and sustained; he added that "conditions for a largely technical exercise such as registration are notably less stringent than those which will be necessary for campaigning in the run-up to the consultation."[10]

The situation of the IDPs, now estimated by UNAMET and UNHCR at some 60,000, remained the biggest uncertainty. The commencement of the registration period had prompted a wide-ranging movement of IDPs. Many returned to their home villages, where they wanted to obtain documentation, register, and vote; others moved into Dili to do so; some continued to be freshly displaced from their villages by recent militia activity. Those who returned to their home districts appeared to be motivated by political factors, encouraged by the CNRT rather than by an assessment that it had become safe for them to do so, although the growing international presence was no doubt a contributory factor. In some cases, they were moving from situations of relative safety into a greater risk of violence and to areas where for security reasons humanitarian aid was not available.

The militia attack on the Liquiça convoy had set back efforts to deliver assistance, although the ensuing publicity had compelled the Indonesian authorities to recognize the humanitarian issue and Habibie had ordered efforts to address it. It continued to be seen as a highly political issue. Not only were the IDPs regarded as undesirable pro-independence elements (the very reason they had been targeted in the first place), but so were the East Timorese NGOs that wished to assist them. The Indonesians saw themselves in a competition to win support by delivering relief through government channels.[11] They therefore sought to coordinate—or control—assistance efforts. UNHCR was recognized as the lead agency, but despite UNHCR's and UNAMET's efforts, the obstacles imposed by the authorities meant that it was not until 2 August—nearly a month after the 4 July Liquiça attack—that another convoy reached one of the major areas of displacement.

What was clear, however, was that despite insecurity and distress, the IDPs in East Timor were managing to register. This was facilitated by a crucial element of the UN's electoral planning, which had anticipated that intimidation would be the main problem to be faced. It had been decided that a voter could register at any registration center of his or her choice, not necessarily at the one nearest to the place of normal residence. (The voter would then have to vote at that same location, so there would be later anxieties at the consequences of continuing displacement.) Some emerged from hiding to register at the nearest center and promptly went back into hiding until they did the same again on polling day.

Special arrangements were made for one small but significant group of voters: East Timorese who were in prison. In this case alone, mobile teams of DEOs were authorized to go to register people unable to present themselves at a registration center. Some 272 prisoners were registered in East Timor. Xanana Gusmão was taken from his detention to register at the Jakarta center. East Timorese serving in the TNI and the police were fully entitled to register but were restricted from carrying guns or appearing in uniform when presenting themselves at the registration center. No special arrangements were made to enable

Falintil fighters to register; UNAMET tried but failed to get a formal undertaking from the Indonesian authorities that they would not be arrested in the process of registering. Some came down from the hills to the nearest registration center, but many felt unable to do so.

EXTENDING REGISTRATION

In addition to those displaced within East Timor, there were substantial numbers of East Timorese who had gone in recent months to West Timor, mostly living near the border, around Atambua. These formed part of a much larger number of people in West Timor who were quali-fied, by parentage if not by birth, to vote in the consultation and who were presumed to be mostly potential pro-autonomy voters. The agree-ments provided for external registration centers at five locations in Indonesia. The locations listed had been provided by the Indonesian negotiators; in retrospect, it is hard to understand how their list had failed to include a location in West Timor.[12] The UN was pressed to add to the external centers, not only by the Indonesian government in rela-tion to West Timor, but also by East Timorese wanting to vote at addi-tional locations in Australia and Europe. It had no resources to allow for centers additional to those that had already been established, in accor-dance with the agreements, by the International Organization for Migration (and in Australia by the Australian Electoral Commission). Although the chosen locations could have been adjusted at the outset within the given total, this was no longer possible by the time requests were made.

It was therefore agreed that UNAMET would reinforce registration centers nearest the border between East and West Timor in Bobonaro and Ambeno districts to accommodate extra numbers of registrants who would be transported there from the west. Additional staff were moved from locations where the numbers were falling below the expected average of 2,000 per center to those where they were likely to exceed substantially the expected maximum of 3,000, and additional materials were put in place. This was necessary to accommodate not only those coming across the border, but also the patterns resulting from internal displacement inside East Timor.

As the end of the twenty-day registration period drew near, UNAMET was satisfied that even the great majority of IDPs had been able to register. The Indonesian efforts to organize the transport of peo-ple from West Timor had, however, got fully under way only late in the process, and this appeared to be the major factor in a strong demand from the Indonesian government for an extension of the period of registration. On 28 July, the Secretary-General had fixed the date of the ballot as 30 August.[13] The Indonesians had been expecting a two-week delay beyond the original ballot date of 8 August and now saw this three-week delay as allowing for a one-week extension of registration. In fact, it was based on the latest calculation of the time required, beyond the end of registration on 4 August, for the computerization of the voter lists, their display, and the opportunity for challenges and their adjudication. There were also CNRT pleas for an extension, although in the end, Gusmão formally requested this only for the external centers in Indonesia, where East Timorese were making arrangements to travel long distances. The CEO saw no objective case for the extension of registration, and the electoral staff in the field would already have worked intensely for twenty long days without any break. But I recommended, and New York agreed, that the registration period should be extended by two days in East Timor—shaving away any remaining leeway in the overall timetable—and by four days at the external centers, to give the travelers one more weekend to reach their destinations. The electoral perspective was fully supported by the fact that already on the last scheduled day, the numbers registering fell away, and only some 6,000 people registered in East Timor in the final two-day extension period. But any possible grievance that people had not had a reasonable opportunity to register was averted, and it is noteworthy that at no time thereafter was any group of persons identified as having been excluded. UNAMET announced that 446,666 people had registered: 433,576 in East Timor itself, and 13,090 at the external centers. When all checks had been completed, the total would rise to 451,792.

THE REGISTER FINALIZED

The registration data were computerized; every fifth day throughout the registration all data were collected in Dili and flown to Sydney, where inputting continued throughout the registration period. This allowed for different checks, in particular to detect multiple registration. Lists of voters, which were produced for each polling station, were displayed for a period of five days, 19–23 August, at all registration centers and at UNAMET's regional offices and Dili headquarters. Challenges to the lists would be adjudicated by the independent Electoral Commission.

The Electoral Commission had been only fleetingly referred to in the agreement on modalities, but the Secretary-General had set out his intention in his 22 May report.[14] He appointed three eminent international experts with notable experience in political conflict: Judge Johann Kriegler (chairperson of the Electoral Commission of South Africa, chosen by his colleagues to chair the commission); Pat Bradley (chief electoral officer for Northern Ireland); and Bong-Scuk Sohn (commissioner of the National Election Commission of the Republic of Korea). These experts had final decisionmaking authority regarding all complaints, challenges, and disputes concerning the consultation and operated as a certifying body for each stage of the process. According to their terms of reference, they were not subject to the direction or control of any person or authority. The CEO could attend and address meetings of the Electoral Commission, and they had access to the SRSG as requested, but they were fully independent of both UNAMET and New York. They had arrived in Dili before or just after the opening of registration and had immediately begun to observe the process at first hand.

The exhibition and objection process was well publicized, but not many East Timorese came to see the lists, and those who did came to verify their own registration. During the registration, there had been only 913 rejections: 105 persons had exercised their right of appeal, and the Electoral Commission had determined 52 in favor of the voter and 53 against. Only 27 objections to the lists were now received in East Timor, all from one district and based on an allegation that the applicants had been West Timorese. The only major objection came from the Indonesian government, alleging that some 700 persons registered in Portugal appeared not to be ethnically East Timorese. However, it was acknowledged that they had fulfilled the criteria for registration, and the commission found no valid basis for the objection, as ethnicity was not a criterion. Indonesia found some agreement from both the Portuguese government and the UN that the participation of ethnic Portuguese was contrary to the intention of the agreements, but the number alleged seemed exaggerated and nothing could be done, given that the UN had applied the criteria correctly.

On 25 August, the Electoral Commission issued its formal determination on the registration of voters. The commission said that it had found the regulatory framework for the consultation and the human and material resources mustered by UNAMET for the job to be excellent. During the registration of voters, the commission had been impressed by "the calm and reassuring atmosphere of competence and determination manifested at registration centers." The exercise was manifestly successful: the register of voters was indeed a sound basis for the conduct of the popular consultation.[15]

TOWARD THE CAMPAIGN

While registration had been proceeding, UNAMET had been seeking responses from the two sides on key elements of preparation for the ballot: the symbols to be reproduced on the ballot papers, and the code of conduct for the campaign. This was somewhat facilitated when the two pro-autonomy groups, the FPDK and the BRTT, came together in the Front Bersama Pro-Otonomi Timor Timur (UNIF; United Front for East Timor Autonomy). The wording of the two options on the ballot paper was laid down in the agreements and was somewhat complex, so symbols designed to facilitate voting by illiterate voters were crucial.[16] The CNRT and UNIF both proposed symbols that made use of an outline map of East Timor with a flag planted upon it: the Indonesian flag for autonomy, and the CNRT flag for independence. Anxieties that these would be so similar as to confuse voters were overcome when UNAMET produced a color representation of the resulting ballot paper. A small pro-independence party outside the CNRT protested at the use of the CNRT flag as the independence symbol, but the ballot was not intended as an election or test of the legitimacy of any organization. After the ballot, however, the votes cast "for the CNRT flag" would indeed be cited as a basis for its legitimacy as the leading representative organization during the transition and prior to elections.

A proposed campaign code of conduct had been drafted by UNAMET, was readily accepted by the CNRT, and was subject to only a small number of requested amendments from UNIF. These gave rise to a series of remarkably cordial and cooperative meetings between UNAMET and the two parties together. On 9 August, UNAMET held a ceremony at which I issued the Code of Conduct for Participants, and leading representatives of UNIF and the CNRT signed it to formalize their acceptance, in the presence of Bishop Belo, representatives of the Indonesian Task Force, Portuguese and Indonesian observation missions, and the chief of police. A sample of the ballot paper, with the final version of the symbols, was unveiled at the same time and henceforth was widely reproduced in UNAMET's own public information and in the campaigns.

The campaign code provided for the freedom for both sides to campaign without disruption or obstruction. It committed participants in the campaigns to avoid inflammatory or defamatory language, to avoid and condemn political violence or intimidation, and not to respond to provocation other than to report it to the Indonesian police. It required all participants to uphold the secrecy of the ballot. The wording to which UNIF was most sensitive in the negotiations was the concluding commitment to accept the result. In the end, UNIF agreed to the wording the pro-autonomy parties had already accepted at the Dare II reconciliation meeting convened by the bishops of East Timor (described in the following chapter): "All the participants agree to accept the officially validated outcome of the popular consultation, in accordance with the Main Agreement of 5 May 1999."

UNAMET was not naïve in its expectations of the effectiveness of the campaign code of conduct amid the prevailing climate. Nor did the CNRT expect it to create the level playing field to which they were entitled. But Gusmão in particular was so convinced of overwhelming majority support for independence that he regarded public campaigning as unnecessary. He was anxious to avoid clashes during the campaign period and to use that time to promote reconciliation for the period ahead. One of the younger-generation activists who was centrally involved in the CNRT campaign describes how Gusmão—who, he says, "was always too optimistic concerning many things"—gave early instructions to leaders of the youth organizations that they were not to respond in kind to the pro-autonomy campaigning, but to go door-to-door in the villages and make people aware of the importance of reconciliation.[17] The major focus of the campaign committee established by the CNRT was informal distribution of the pro-independence symbol and explanation of the voting procedures, carried out on the model of previous clandestine work.[18] Only a limited number of public pro-independence rallies were planned.

UNAMET established regional campaign committees to promote the observance of the campaign code, some equalization of campaign opportunities, and the avoidance of violent clashes. As defined in a formal Notification of the CEO, these committees were to be chaired by UNAMET's regional electoral coordinator and to comprise representatives of the two sides and of the Indonesian police, as well as UNAMET's political officer and CIVPOL. In Dili and some other regions, it was agreed to allocate alternate days for campaigning by the opposing sides. UNAMET regarded the ability of the CNRT to establish offices as a minimum indicator of security. Before the campaign opened on 14 August, CNRT offices had at last been opened in Dili, Baucau, Manatuto, Lautem, Viqueque, and Cova Lima districts. Only during the campaign period would Ainaro, Ambeno, Aileu, and Manufahi be added to the list; in three districts—Bobonaro, Ermera, and Liquiça—they were never able to open, and several of those that did open would soon be destroyed or closed.

Gusmão had even at one stage proposed a "joint campaign," in which pro-autonomy and pro-independence representatives would tour

the territory to present together their views and their support for reconciliation whatever the outcome. This was not accepted by the pro-autonomy side, but they did agree to a joint launching of the campaign. The
agreements had prescribed a seventeen-day campaign period, followed
by a two-day cooling-off period before the ballot. With the poll on 30
August, this would have begun on 11 August, but in view of the extension of registration, the parties agreed to shorten this to fourteen days.
On 14 August, in another ceremony at UNAMET's headquarters, representatives of the CNRT and UNIF launched the campaign.

NOTES

1. The third case of the UN organizing a ballot was in Eastern Slavonia
in 1996.

2. A detailed operational account of the electoral aspects of UNAMET is
contained in *East Timor Popular Consultation: Electoral Operations Report,*
November 1999, prepared by UNAMET's Electoral Unit. I have drawn on this
throughout, especially in this chapter and in Chapter 7.

3. Though owned by a prominent pro-integration East Timorese who was
one of the founders of the BRTT, *Suara Timor Timur* had previously been
attacked by militia for being too balanced in its reporting and was to be a target
again in the postballot destruction.

4. See David Wimhurst, "The United Nations Information Intervention in
East Timor," in Monroe E. Price and Mark Thompson, eds., *Forging Peace:
International Intervention, Media and Conflict* (Edinburgh: Edinburgh
University Press, forthcoming).

5. *Report of the Secretary-General,* S/1999/803, 20 July 1999.

6. Yayasan HAK, Committee for a Free and Fair Ballot, Report No. 2,
Violations in the Registration of the Ballot, 26 July 1999.

7. Carter Center, Reports on East Timor Nos. 1 and 2, reproduced in
Observing the 1999 Public Consultation Process in East Timor: Final Report,
Atlanta, June 2000. Available online at http://www.Cartercenter.org/
COUNTRIES/etimor.html; and International Federation for East Timor
Observer Project, Report No. 2, *Tens of Thousands of Voters Register Amidst
Persistent Pockets of Intimidation,* 23 July 1999.

8. For a firsthand account by a DEO, see Catharina Williams,
"Experiences of a District Electoral Officer in Suai," in James J. Fox and
Dionisio Babo Soares, eds., *Out of the Ashes: The Destruction and
Reconstruction of East Timor* (London: C. Hurst, 2000).

9. Letter dated 26 July 1999 from the Secretary-General addressed to the
President of the Security Council, S/1999/822.

10. Ibid.

11. This is explicit in the Garnadi memorandum referred to in Chapter 6.

12. The locations were Jakarta, Yogyakarta, Surabaya, Denpasar, and
Ujung Pandang.

13. Letter dated 28 July 1999 from the Secretary-General addressed to the
President of the Security Council, S/1999/830.

14. *Report of the Secretary-General,* S/1999/595, 22 May 1999, par. 14.

15. Electoral Commission, East Timor Popular Consultation, *Determination: Registration of Voters,* 25 August 1999.

16. For quotation of the two options, see Chapter 2, p. 28.

17. Fernando de Araujo, "The CNRT Campaign for Independence," in Fox and Babo Soares, eds., *Out of the Ashes,* pp. 100–101.

18. Ibid., p. 107.

5

Reconciliation and the Laying Down of Arms

FROM DARE II TO THE EAST TIMORESE CONSULTATIVE COMMISSION

The UN recognized from the outset that not only the peaceful conduct of the ballot, but even more the success of the transition to follow it, depended on the willingness of the East Timorese to overcome past divisions. These went back to the first formation of political parties in 1974 and the killings by both sides in 1975. While some East Timorese leaders had been consistent in their opposition to or support for integration with Indonesia, the allegiances of others had shifted. Prominent figures on both sides in 1999 had switched their support from integration to independence, or vice versa. Close family relationships crossed the political divide. Some interpreted this optimistically; the East Timorese could transcend their divisions if these were no longer deliberately exploited by Indonesia. The Indonesians expressed the pessimistic view: the East Timorese were culturally predisposed to bitter division and violent conflict.

Since 1995, the UN had been bringing together East Timorese leaders in the annual All-Inclusive Intra–East Timorese Dialogue (AIETD).[1] Held at two Austrian castles, it was an unusual, far-sighted initiative, for which the UN had to beg special funding from interested governments. The Indonesian insistence that the AIETD should not discuss the political status of East Timor limited its formal outcome. But it enabled the UN to build relationships with the East Timorese and, more important, it brought together those in exile and those inside, albeit without the key presence of Gusmão.

As the expectations and tension mounted after the fall of Suharto and Habibie's offer of autonomy, Bishop Belo and his colleague,

Bishop Basilio do Nascimento of Baucau, convoked a meeting of East Timorese leaders in September 1998 to facilitate dialogue and foster reconciliation among them. It took place at Dare, the location in the hills above Dili of the seminary at which many of them had been educated. It was followed not by reconciliation but by the violence of early 1999. With the signing of the agreements, the bishops were ready to try again, and they worked with international specialists in conflict resolution toward convening a Dare II. UNAMET gave quiet support to the practical arrangements for the bishops' separate meetings with representatives of the two sides that laid the groundwork for the full conference.

The Dare II Peace and Reconciliation Meeting itself took place in Jakarta from 25 to 30 June 1999. The location allowed the participation of Gusmão, and the Indonesian government issued visas to all the pro-independence exiles chosen to participate, including Ramos-Horta. Gusmão was able to meet the latter, and others who had been Fretilin's and later the CNRT's external representatives, for the first time since 1975. Outside the meeting itself, the old adversaries, Alatas and Ramos-Horta, met in a noncombative spirit for the first time, and both the Habibie government and the CNRT displayed considerable statesmanship.

The Dare II conference itself was, however, a disappointment to the bishops, and despite discussions conducted in a good atmosphere, it ended on a subdued note.[2] It agreed on a statement of "points of convergence," including disarmament of the militias and of Falintil and respect for the outcome of the popular consultation. Pro-independence delegates failed to get consensus support for the release of Gusmão to take part in campaigning. Pro-autonomy delegates pressed their view that wide-ranging autonomy was already a concession by the integrationists—one that should be matched by concessions on the pro-independence side; they pressed for "more assurance of neutrality" on the part of UNAMET. The key failure was that although both sides accepted the crucial need for further dialogue, they were unable to agree on a procedure to carry the talks forward. After an appeal by Bishop Nascimento for "real substance," a joint commission had been proposed as a follow-up, but the pro-autonomy representatives withheld consent. Gusmão was convinced that, on this and other occasions, a willingness to go further that he found in his direct discussions with pro-autonomy leaders did not survive their reporting back to Indonesian authorities.

The bishops concluded that they could do nothing more to take the Dare process forward before the ballot. It now fell to the UN to do what it could. The agreements provided that in the event of a transition to autonomy, a broadly representative transitional council of up to twenty-five East Timorese, appointed after consultation by the UN Secretary-General, would operate until elections had been held. Whatever the outcome of the ballot, it would be even more crucial for the UN to have a group of responsible East Timorese leaders drawn from the two sides to work with in the period up to the MPR decision, which it was well recognized would be the period carrying the greatest risk of violence.

The UN veterans of the AIETD, Vendrell (now designated Deputy Personal Representative of the Secretary-General for East Timor) and Samuel, facilitated an unpublicized meeting with East Timorese leaders on 11 August. It was held in UN premises in Jakarta, so that Gusmão could participate, with equal representation of the two sides. The Indonesian government was informed that the UN's main objective was to achieve agreement on an East Timorese consultative council, with the aim of ensuring that both the "winning" and "losing" sides would have a postballot role whatever the outcome. Jakarta gave its support to this.

The meeting agreed that the behavior and activities of the leaders would be crucial in affecting the reaction of the people to the result of the ballot. The result should be seen not as an exclusive victory for one side, but rather as the expression of the wish of the East Timorese people; there should, said Gusmão, be "no winners and no losers, no heroes and no traitors." An East Timorese Council would be selected to be launched on 31 August, the day after the vote, and would be responsible for fostering reconciliation and cooperation until the start of the implementation of the result of the consultation, after the legislative implementation of separation or autonomy. The council would have twenty-five members, each side nominating ten, with the UN Secretary-General appointing the other five after consultation with Indonesia, Portugal, and the two sides. It would issue an immediate statement on 31 August to promote reconciliation and stability and then convene a broader meeting of East Timorese leaders to promote a smooth transition. On the proposal of pro-autonomy leader Lopes da Cruz, the meeting recommended the early release of Gusmão, not later than the beginning of the campaign period.

The two sides came to a second meeting on 22 August, also in Jakarta, with their nominations for the members of the body. It was now agreed that it would be called the East Timorese Consultative Commission, conforming to an Indonesian request to avoid confusion with the transitional council required by the autonomy proposal. The process for drafting the 31 August statement was decided. The atmosphere of discussion between the political leaders seemed propitious, and the second meeting was attended by two key militia commanders,

Eurico Guterres of Dili and Joanico Cesario Belo of Baucau, who had long discussions with Gusmão in the margins of the meeting. Guterres was participating across the table from Manuel Carrascalão, who held him responsible for the murder of his son in the 17 April attack on his house. In the context of a resurgence of violence in East Timor, and with only eight days to go before the vote, the meeting also discussed how to promote the implementation of the repeated agreements that had by then been reached on the laying down of arms.

THE LAYING DOWN OF ARMS

Despite the UN's view that security for the popular consultation required the laying down of arms by all armed groups and redeployment of the TNI, the 5 May Agreement on security had done no more than pass the responsibility to the Commission on Peace and Stability (KPS), which had finally been established on 21 April.[3] It merely stated that "the Commission, in cooperation with the United Nations, will elaborate a code of conduct, by which all parties should abide, for the period prior to and following the consultation, ensure the laying down of arms and take the necessary steps to achieve disarmament." But the KPS was fatally flawed from its inception. The composition was heavily weighted toward the Indonesian authorities and pro-autonomy representatives; the conveners from Komnas HAM for the most part acted as their surrogates; Falintil was not present; the UN was not always even informed of meetings and was deliberately excluded from the proper involvement that alone could have given the KPS credibility with the CNRT/Falintil.

The meetings of the KPS in Dili were clearly futile, and UNAMET urged that if Gusmão was not permitted to travel elsewhere, the KPS must meet in Jakarta, where he could participate as commander of Falintil as well as president of the CNRT. Eventually this happened. In a key meeting on 18 June, Gusmão and Leandro Isaac, for the CNRT and Falintil, and Domingos Soares of the FPDK and João Tavares as "Commander-in-chief of the Pro-Integration [Forces]" signed a joint agreement and appeal. The crucial provision was that supporters of both sides would cease all acts of violence and surrender all types of weapons to the authorities. However, Gusmão immediately made clear, in a meeting with Wiranto and publicly, that the mechanism for overseeing the disarmament process had yet to be decided and required UN involvement, and that the TNI must be confined to barracks and its village posts closed down.[4] Samuel, who represented UNAMET at the meeting, reported an unmistakable effort on the part of the TNI and pro-autonomy representatives to sideline the UN and to avoid any commitment that would restrict the TNI presence or movements in East Timor, although only this would make effective the responsibility of the Indonesian police for security required by the agreements.

The numbers of police had been steadily increased, from around 3,000 when UNAMET arrived to some 8,000 by August. Wiranto's reaction to each round of international pressure regarding the security situation had been to promise more police. Many were drawn from Indonesia's paramilitary riot police, Brimob, and few were well trained or motivated for the task in East Timor. But more significant than the limitations of their training was their inhibition at acting in the presence of the TNI against militia that were supported by, and included members of, the military. The police were rumored to include TNI soldiers within their ranks and elements of Komando Pasuka Khusus (Kopassus; Indonesian Army Special Forces Command) in Brimob uniforms, an allegation quietly confirmed by some Indonesian police to colleagues in UNAMET CIVPOL, whom they began to regard as colleagues. The withdrawal of the TNI from the districts would have been crucial to a more independent police role. The numbers of TNI were never notified to UNAMET; it was a constant source of frustration to the chief military liaison officer (CMLO) that the TNI would not even inform the MLOs of their current troop strength and deployment. But UNAMET believed that they were in excess of 15,000, and at no stage was there any indication of a significant reduction.

This began an impasse that would never be resolved. The TNI consistently presented the issue as one of mutual disarmament of Falintil and the militia. The militia, they claimed, existed only because of the Falintil threat. But for Falintil, it was the Indonesian army that they had fought against for twenty-four years, and the militia were merely its creation. Gusmão's minimum position was a reduction of the TNI forces in East Timor and their confinement to district-level barracks, in which context Falintil could surrender weapons to the UN. Even this would have put his authority to a severe test; for most of Falintil, it was unthinkable that they would disarm as long as the TNI remained in East Timor.

The KPS began a series of local visits to publicize the 18 June appeal and thus calm the situation in the districts. But it was clear that the laying down of arms, and certainly disarmament, would not proceed until there was further agreement on the extent of deployment of the TNI and the modalities for verification and handover of weapons. The conveners of the KPS made no move to commence discussion of these issues. Wiranto pushed for the disarmament of Falintil. On 7 July, he told me and Vendrell, as he had told others, that if Falintil was ready to surrender its weapons to the Indonesian police, he could guarantee that the militia would be disarmed within two days. The TNI, however, evaded discussion of their own redeployment. Gusmão urged the UN to define and decide on a body that would supervise and monitor the disarmament process, other than the Indonesian police, and suggested that this required an international military authority. But DPKO advised that the UN's experience from elsewhere taught that supervising disarmament required substantial troop strength, and it was far beyond UNAMET's mandate, resources, or timescale. I responded to Gusmão that deciding on a mechanism for disarmament had never been regarded as a UN matter; that decision had to result from discussions between the relevant parties, with UNAMET's involvement. Given the continuing failure of the KPS to address the outstanding issues, I proposed that UNAMET should organize meetings between CNRT/Falintil and the TNI on the one hand, and CNRT/Falintil and militia leaders on the other.

Gusmão agreed and had meanwhile decided to order a unilateral cantonment of Falintil forces. The Indonesians consistently presented the militia and their actions as a response to threatened or actual pro-independence violence and criticized UN statements for not being even-handed when they described the militia as overwhelmingly the main perpetrators of violence during the UNAMET presence. Yet this was the reality. Whatever may have preceded its arrival, UNAMET observed that Falintil exercised great discipline in the face of militia violence. UNAMET sought to investigate alleged Falintil abuses but they were only occasionally substantiated; it did participate in the release of persons held hostage by Falintil. The small number of killings that could have been attributable to pro-independence perpetrators rarely appeared to be carried out by Falintil fighters themselves. They thus frustrated the apparent TNI strategy of drawing them into open conflict with the militia, in order to substantiate the continuing Indonesian claim that the conflict was one among Timorese factions, necessitating the TNI's security presence. But Gusmão was concerned that following the 18 June KPS agreement, Falintil was nevertheless repeatedly accused of being the obstacle to disarmament. He hoped that deciding on unilateral cantonment as a mechanism for disarmament would make clear that Falintil was not the source of violence and would put pressure on the TNI and the militia to reciprocate. Falintil would be grouped in four cantonment sites and would not move out of them with weapons; UNAMET's MLOs would be invited to confirm this. On 26 July, UNAMET's CMLO, with a KPS representative, met for the first time

Falintil's deputy commander, Taur Matan Ruak, at the initial cantonment site at Uai Mori (Viqueque district). By 12 August, Falintil achieved their final cantonment, declaring to the visiting MLOs a disposition of 260 guerrillas at Uai Mori, 70 at Atalari (Baucau), 153 at Poetete (Ermera), and 187 at Aiassa (Bobonaro).

At the end of July, the TNI, in the person of regional commander Damiri, promised UNAMET that if Falintil carried out its cantonment, the TNI would pull back to the subdistrict or district level and keep weapons under strict guard; the militia would also concentrate forces and safeguard weapons. Immediately after the publicity given to the completion of Falintil's cantonment, militia leaders announced their own intention to lay down arms. Now calling themselves Pasukan Pejuang Integrasi (PPI; Integration Struggle Troops), the militia presented and secured weapons at parades in Atabae, Bobonaro district (16 August); Cassa, Ainaro district (18 August); and Baucau and Dili (both 19 August). The number of weapons laid down was obviously only a fraction of those in possession of the militia; unlike Falintil the militia did not remain in cantonment areas, and the rhetoric that UNAMET's MLOs had to listen to on parade was hardly encouraging. At the Cassa parade, Mahidi leader Cancio de Carvalho declared that the "wrong choice" in the ballot would lead to war in East Timor and that those who chose wrongly would suffer the consequences. But for UNAMET, the significant issue was not the credibility of "cantonment" in itself but whether the Indonesian police would now act against those who were still flourishing weapons and would be supported in doing so rather than inhibited by the TNI. There was no sign that the TNI itself was preparing to pull back to barracks.

THE RELEASE OF XANANA GUSMÃO

One man was central to the management of the situation in East Timor before and after the ballot. Xanana Gusmão was not only the acknowledged leader of all the pro-independence groups gathered together in the CNRT; he was the commander in chief of Falintil, with whom he had fought for seventeen years until his capture in 1992. At the same time, he was the independence leader most determined and best able to reach out to his East Timorese political opponents; and, through his imprisonment in Jakarta, he had a keen sense of Indonesia's democratic evolution. While deeply mistrustful of the Indonesian military's motives and conduct in East Timor, he spoke openly of the need to enable them to withdraw with honor.

The UN-led pressure on Indonesia to release Gusmão and engage him in serious dialogue had for years received little response. Jakarta maintained that he was a common criminal with whom there was little to discuss, although Nelson Mandela's successful request to see him when he visited Indonesia in July 1997 brought him further into the international arena and encouraged later diplomatic visitors. As the negotiations progressed, Jakarta promised to release him as part of the overall settlement but appeared to want to use his release to obtain concessions from Portugal. The Secretary-General welcomed his January 1999 transfer from Cipinang prison to a prison house, an important concession that improved access to him for the UN, other diplomats, and those East Timorese who could travel to Jakarta. This had been suggested by Jamsheed Marker, who in response to the contention that Indonesian law made no provision for house arrest, had cited the precedent of British detention of Mahatma Gandhi in a residence, after declaring it officially a prison.[5] But his detention in Jakarta was still a major limitation to the role he could have played in East Timor itself. In late June, Marker began to press more insistently on behalf of the Secretary-General for Gusmão's release. The UN was concerned that the popular consultation could not be regarded as fully fair if the leader of one side was still detained during the campaign. But of still greater practical concern was the role the UN felt Gusmão could play in helping to stabilize the situation in East Timor; we believed that his direct participation was needed in the efforts toward reconciliation and the laying down of arms. At key moments, progress was made only when Gusmão was present at meetings, and the fact that these had to take place in Jakarta slowed the pace of negotiations and temporarily removed other key actors from fast-moving developments in East Timor.

The formal Indonesian response was in part founded on their view of the propriety of Gusmão's criminal conviction, although their long-standing position that he would be released only as part of an overall settlement was reflected in a promise that this would come immediately after the ballot. But privately Habibie insisted that he had reason to fear for Gusmão's safety if he were returned to East Timor. This insistence was maintained in the face of the UN's final preballot representations, when UNAMET saw Gusmão's presence in Dili as a key factor that could enhance the ability of the East Timorese Consultative Commission to face the challenge of violence after the vote. In the light of subsequent events, it is hard to dismiss the alleged threat to his life had he been allowed to return before the ballot.

RESURGENCE OF VIOLENCE

As the campaign period began, some optimism could be derived from the cooperation of the leaderships over the campaign code of conduct, their agreement in Jakarta to prepare for the transition, the joint campaign launch, the establishment of regional campaign committees and the opening of CNRT offices, and some apparent momentum toward the laying down of arms. The tripartite talks in Jakarta in mid-August had seen the Indonesian side promising cooperation and apparently facing up to the possibility of a defeat for the autonomy proposal. When Marker traveled on to visit East Timor, he was upbeat about the commitment of the Indonesian government to a peaceful process. But UNAMET's warning to New York that the fundamentals of insecurity had not been addressed and that apparent improvements could quickly be reversed was soon borne out.

Activities that demonstrated the strength of support for independence, and in particular the presence of students who had returned from Indonesia or Dili to work in the districts, were taken as provocative. Even before the opening of the campaign, incidents between students and militia in Viqueque led to heavy shooting by the TNI and militia, with two students dead. The information center established by the East Timor Student Solidarity Council was attacked, the CNRT office was destroyed only eight days after it had opened, and independence leaders fled the town. Just at the time when the militia were supposedly laying down their arms, the visible presence, threats, and violence of armed militia groups were in fact intensifying in almost all districts. Fully-armed militia participated in pro-autonomy rallies, while attacks on CNRT activists multiplied. More CNRT offices were attacked before the last of them had opened: in Dili on 17 August, Manatuto on 19 August, and Ainaro on 21 August. In Bobonaro, the *bupati* had resisted any CNRT activity, and even the theoretical regional campaign agreement allocated only one-quarter of campaigning days to the CNRT and three-quarters to three pro-autonomy groups; on 18 August, an influx of militia groups into Maliana town sparked a day of violence in which the students' office was targeted, at least one student killed, and the UNAMET office seriously threatened. In Cova Lima district, militia activities led to an increase in the number of IDPs in the church compound at Suai; a pro-independence activist was kidnapped and murdered, and after a clash between militia and pro-independence supporters waiting to leave for a campaign rally on 19 August, the CNRT suspended its activities. The overall CNRT campaign culminated in a well-attended peaceful rally in Dili on 25 August. But the final day allocated to the pro-autonomy campaign, 26 August, became the occasion for militia groups, many from outside Dili, to roam around the city unhindered, commandeering vehicles. At least six people were killed, one of them a militia member; but the others were apparently killed by militia, and many were wounded. The main CNRT office was sacked and looted by militia, the Indonesian police failing to intervene. On the very last day of the campaign, militia rampaged through a village in Maliana, killing three people; and in Lospalos, hitherto one of the least-troubled places, the pro-independence *liurai* (traditional leader) was killed in the compound where he had allowed the CNRT to have its office. UNAMET's CIVPOL believed that his military-style killing had the hallmarks of a Kopassus operation.

LAST EFFORTS

UNAMET intensified its efforts to persuade the TNI to avert further violence. On 13 August, a new military commander for East Timor, Colonel Mohamad Noer Muis, took over from Suratman. The change was announced as routine, and Suratman was promoted to brigadier general. But privately, Indonesian representatives told the UN that this change and the replacement of three district commanders were in response to the concerns of the international community. Certainly the arrival of an officer who had served with the UN, and who at least had not presided over the creation of the militia and their rampages of the first five months of 1999, was assumed to be a positive development.

    I asked the head of the Indonesian Task Force, Tarmidzi, to visit Viqueque, Suai, and Maliana with me to hear UNAMET's briefing on the seriousness of the situations there in the presence of the district military and police chiefs. In Maliana, on 18 August, our helicopter landed in the midst of a town, deserted except for bands of armed militia, to find UNAMET staff and journalists besieged in the UNAMET office. The briefings made clear to the Indonesian Task Force that the levels of insecurity were patently unacceptable for the consultation and that the local authorities were contributing to rather than addressing the impunity of the militia, some of whom were serving members of the TNI. I called publicly for the removal of members of the TNI who had been most closely and obviously associated with the militia. UNAMET had repeatedly given the names of such men to different levels of the chain of command, but I now wrote to Tarmidzi and CMLO Rezaq to Zacky, listing names that included the district commanders in Bobonaro and Cova Lima.

Tarmidzi reported to Jakarta and was called there to brief ministers,[6] while Zacky and Muis went to Maliana, announcing measures that included the control (but not removal) of TNI sergeants who were also local militia leaders and promising to return to ensure follow-through in three days. On the same day, UNAMET DEOs were caught up in a militia attack on students and subsequent clashes between militia and some of the IDPs at the Suai church compound. The local authorities told the priest that the IDPs should leave and had the water supply to over 2,000 IDPs turned off. It took extraordinary efforts by UNAMET and the intervention of a visiting U.S. congressional delegation to get the water turned back on. The gap between the stated intentions of the government in Jakarta and the reality in East Timor had become more glaring than ever. The U.S. delegation's angry report to Habibie in Jakarta led him to order the withdrawal of Zacky, and the Bobonaro and Cova Lima district commanders were at last replaced. However, Zacky reappeared in Maliana on 28 August, and the Bobonaro commander was seen again in the postballot violence there, casting doubt on whether their roles were effectively ended.

Wiranto's intelligence adviser, Rear Admiral Yoost Mengko, and Muis had become UNAMET's main TNI interlocutors in our efforts to promote TNI, Falintil, and militia commitments to the laying down of arms. Mengko, Gusmão, and I met in Jakarta in mid-August. Gusmão had proposed a sequence of meetings: between Wiranto's representative and himself; then between Falintil Deputy Commander Ruak and the East Timor TNI commander; then between regional commanders of Falintil and the PPI. Gusmão and militia leaders Eurico Guterres and Joanico Cesario agreed on a meeting of the four regional commanders on both sides, aimed at producing a common position declaring that anyone carrying weapons outside cantonment areas should be arrested. With less than a week to go to the ballot, UNAMET brought Ruak from Falintil's cantonment in the hills to meet Muis at UNAMET's Dili headquarters on 24 August; UNAMET then flew Mengko and two generals to meet Ruak and the Falintil command at Uai Mori.[7] The meeting of regional commanders, scheduled for 27 August in Dili and nearly derailed by the previous day's violence there, took place on 28 August in Baucau. They agreed that both the PPI and Falintil would order their forces not to carry or use weapons outside each party's designated cantonment sites and called on the Indonesian police to arrest any of their members carrying weapons in contravention of these orders.

Immediately after the ballot, they would conduct mutual visits to the cantonment sites and would discuss the formation of a verification committee to oversee the laying down of arms. The KPS, UNAMET, and the Indonesian police were requested to observe cantonment and the laying down of arms.

The agreement reached in Baucau was made public at an extraordinary ceremony at UNAMET's headquarters the next morning, the day before the ballot. Falintil commanders, helicoptered by UNAMET from their cantonments to Dili, and militia representatives embraced each other in front of the cameras of the world's media and pledged their commitment to the agreement. Police chief Silaen declared that the Indonesian police would take strong action to arrest those with weapons and confiscate arms. Muis promised the TNI's full support.

It was far from the disarmament of militia forces and confinement to designated areas of Falintil and TNI one month before the ballot, which the UN had originally proposed as the requirement for the consultation. But it was the most UNAMET could achieve. It was not enough.

NOTES

1. See Chapter 2, p. 19.
2. Dare II Steering Committee press release, *Dare II Talks End on a Subdued Note,* 30 June 1999.
3. See Chapter 2, p. 30.
4. Press release, *A Step Towards Peace in East Timor,* 18 June 1999.
5. Jamsheed Marker, *Quiet Diplomacy: A Personal Memoire of the East Timor Negotiations* (forthcoming), chap. 11.
6. There is an account of the resulting discussion in Don Greenlees and Robert Garran, *East Timor* (Crows Nest, NSW: Allen and Unwin, forthcoming), chap. 8.
7. Major Generals Kiki Syahnakri and Sjafrie Sjamsoeddin.

6

Looking Ahead

PLANNING BEYOND THE BALLOT

While UNAMET was struggling to implement the popular consultation on the ground in East Timor, UN headquarters in New York had begun to look beyond the ballot. The consultation itself was Phase I of the UN role; thereafter it was to be planned in two further phases. Phase II would be the period between the ballot and the implementation of the result, requiring action by the Indonesian legislature either to establish the Special Autonomous Region of East Timor or to repeal the 1976 law purporting to incorporate East Timor into Indonesia and hand over authority to the UN. Phase III would be the period of implementing either the autonomy plan or the transition to independence.

In mid-July, the UN presented a discussion paper to a meeting with senior officials of the Indonesian and Portuguese governments, describing in general terms the role the UN would envisage playing under each of the possible scenarios. The paper assumed that Indonesia would maintain responsibility for security throughout Phase II and until a handover to UN authority if the vote had been for independence. Designed to open a constructive discussion with Indonesia, it did not yet make specific proposals for the numbers or mandate of UN civilian police and military during Phase II. In the meeting, it was recognized that there was a serious danger of conflict once the result of the ballot was announced, as a consequence of the possible refusal of the "losing" side to abide by the outcome of the vote. The UN's efforts (described in the previous chapter) to initiate a dialogue among key East Timorese leaders from both sides about the transition and to form the nucleus of a consultative body were endorsed. It was agreed in principle that after the ballot, UNAMET would have a modified mandate, with a civilian component (minus most of the electoral personnel), a CIVPOL component, and a strengthened military component.

Planning and discussions about the military and police presence in Phase II continued in New York, in consultation with UNAMET's CMLO and Police Commissioner and their staffs. The UN proposed that the CIVPOL strength be increased from the maximum of 280 initially authorized for UNAMET to around 400, with an additional fifty trainers for the new East Timorese police. The military liaison component should evolve into a military observer component and be strengthened to give it a capacity for patrolling. But throughout the discussions, Indonesia remained adamant that it would remain in full control of security during Phase II and rejected any suggestion of an expanded role for the UN until after the formal MPR decision, even if the autonomy proposal had been rejected. It would not accept that the UN military and police should be mandated to "monitor" the roles of the TNI and Indonesian police and insisted that the military component continue to operate as military liaison officers under the existing mandate rather than becoming military observers with a capacity to patrol. When on 9 August the Secretary-General put to the Security Council the UN's proposals for restructuring UNAMET after the ballot, he proposed 410 CIVPOL plus about fifty trainers and 300 military liaison officers, with no change in their mandate.[1] The Indonesians complained that they had not agreed in advance to the latter figure but eventually accepted it.

During these negotiations, UNAMET impressed upon New York the seriousness of its concern regarding the likelihood of violence immediately following the announcement of the outcome of the ballot and argued for the strongest and most visible uniformed UN presence in the immediate postballot period that could be achieved. It was stressing in its public information the UN's commitment to remain after the ballot; it was therefore particularly concerned that there would, in fact, be an immediate reduction in its presence as the electoral staff were repatriated and the CIVPOL were pulled back from 200 polling centers to operate from thirteen regional centers. It therefore argued for the increased numbers of CIVPOL and MLOs to be deployed to East Timor before the vote—so that they were on the ground for the most difficult period—and for some of the UN Volunteers, who as DEOs had become a familiar and reassuring presence in the countryside, to stay on in the new civil affairs component.

The retention of some eighty of the UNVs was agreed, but New York told UNAMET that it was unrealistic to expect deployment of additional CIVPOL before the ballot. Security Council authorization and allocation of funds would be required, and this would have to wait until the U.S. government had consulted Congress. It was thus only on 27 August—three days before the ballot—that the Council authorized the reconfiguration of UNAMET for Phase II.[2] The Secretary-General's report had warned the Council that during the interim phase between the conclusion of the popular consultation and the start of the implementation of its result, the situation in East Timor would be "rather delicate." Already in early August, UNAMET had put it more starkly to New York: the Council needed to be aware that if the Indonesians did not or could not guarantee the security situation, in a context of demoralization of their security forces and civilian officials, the Council would be faced with a major problem in guaranteeing the safety of UN personnel and the population in general in East Timor.

PREDICTIONS AND PRESSURES

As the day of the ballot drew nearer, while current violence escalated, threats and predictions proliferated of still greater violence ahead. These were not new; back in May, Suratman had declared:

> There will be a civil war which I imagine will be much worse and more horrifying than in 1975. If the pro-independents do win, it won't just be the government of Indonesia that has to deal with what follows. The UN and Australia are also going to have to solve the problem. And well if this does happen then there'll be no winners, everything is going to be destroyed. East Timor won't exist as it does now. It'll be much worse than 23 years ago.[3]

Now the warnings took the forms of the public pronouncements of militia leaders, of the private intelligence brought to UNAMET about plans being made and weapons distributed, and of the analysis of developments in some districts by UNAMET's own political officers. Some of the reported plans were of violence to disrupt the ballot, before or on polling day; others were of a full-scale offensive after the vote should the autonomy option be defeated. In Bobonaro district in particular, there were persistent reports of plans to seal the district with roadblocks, shut down the electricity supply, and attack independence supporters. UNAMET's political officers in Bobonaro and Cova Lima were uncertain that the ballot could go ahead in these districts and warned that immediate and firm measures were required to avert war and humanitarian crisis after the ballot. The humanitarian affairs officer reported on the new movement of IDPs resulting from the escalation of violence. He foresaw the likelihood of major displacement after the ballot, with pro-autonomy supporters and non–East Timorese moving into West Timor and others fleeing to forest areas, Falintil cantonments, and places of potential protection.

UNAMET had for some time been aware of preparations to receive large numbers of displaced persons in West Timor. A significant insight into Indonesian thinking was gained in July, when a confidential memorandum came into the possession of journalists.[4] Dated 3 July and titled "General Assessment If Option 1 Fails," it was addressed to the coordinating minister for political and security affairs, Feisal Tanjung, by a senior member of his team in Dili, Major General (retired) H. R. Garnadi. Its authenticity was denied by the spokesperson of the Indonesian Task Force, but in forwarding it to New York, UNAMET was inclined to believe it to be authentic. The writer of the memorandum declared that Indonesia had been left behind in the effort to win the hearts of the people, and while there was still time to confront the situation, "time is running out, without any sign of hope for a victory for Option 1 [autonomy]." A contingency plan in case of independence must therefore be developed, including an evacuation of all civil servants and migrants to West Timor.[5] Nearer the date of the ballot, Zacky and Muis told UNAMET of preparations for evacuations, and Muis and the state secretary and minister for justice, Muladi, were quoted on the issue in the press, the latter referring to the "strong possibility" of an exodus of about 223,000 people if the independence option were chosen.[6] But there was nothing unexpected or inherently unreasonable about contingency plans for departing Indonesians and pro-integrationists; those plans did not imply the coerced removal of people who would wish to stay in East Timor after the ballot.

It was not easy to know how to assess the threats and reported plans of violence. Ever since its arrival in East Timor, UNAMET had been deluged with reports of TNI and militia meetings allegedly planning specific acts of violence, against independence supporters and against UNAMET itself. Almost none had taken place as predicted, and they had provided little reliable guidance to the violence that had occurred. The threats that intensified as the ballot drew near clearly represented a final effort to intimidate voters into opting for autonomy, but would they be carried out if they failed to achieve this? Violence to disrupt the ballot or wreak vengeance afterward might well be being planned by militia and elements within the TNI, but UNAMET had seen militia violence rise and fall in response to political pressure on the TNI leadership. Would the TNI chain of command unleash or control the violence now threatened?

The Habibie government, including Wiranto, had displayed considerable sensitivity to international pressure. The visit to Dili of a large delegation of ministers that had apparently calmed the situation before the opening of registration in July was repeated on 7 August. Marker and I received positive commitments when we met Habibie, Wiranto, and Alatas in Jakarta on 11–12 August. At the tripartite senior officials' meeting on 12–13 August, Indonesia was firm in the commitment that, should the autonomy proposal be rejected—a prospect with which the negotiating officials seemed to have come to terms—it would ensure peace, stability, and the proper functioning of local administration and public services in East Timor until the orderly transfer of authority to the UN. Alatas continued to state this publicly and repeatedly. The Indonesians even indicated at one stage that the government would continue its budgetary support to East Timor until the end of the fiscal year in March 2000. The change in military command in Dili seemed encouraging, although UNAMET continued to report that there had been no change in the fundamentals of the TNI-militia relationship on the ground.

As the violence escalated again from mid-August, so did the international pressure. UNAMET's own efforts to confront the Indonesian Task Force with the full reality have been described in the previous chapter. The impact on the head of the Indonesian Task Force was real and conveyed by him to Jakarta. At the same time, UNAMET reported on the violence and the TNI-militia relationship in strong terms to New York and to its direct diplomatic contacts; Australia and the United States were in any case particularly well informed. An important intervention, confirming but adding weight to UNAMET's own political reporting, came from the independent Electoral Commission. On 20 August, they addressed a letter to me, as the Secretary-General's representative, stating that at no stage had they sensed an atmosphere in East Timor that could be described as "free of intimidation, violence or interference" (the requirements of the agreements), and that "the security situation in East Timor is deteriorating by the day and the lawlessness of the militias increases in intensity, distribution and brazenness." They warned that unless there were significant and remedial action on the part of the Indonesian government, they would have to hold that it had failed to meet its obligations under the agreements and "may be obliged to conclude that such failure resulted in a perversion of the poll in favor of the pro-autonomy camp." The Electoral Commission asked that their views be drawn to the urgent attention of the Secretary-General; they were also conveyed to the Indonesian government both by me through the Indonesian Task Force and in New York by the Secretariat to the Permanent Representative of Indonesia, and were cited when the Secretariat briefed the Security Council on 24 August.

Prior to that briefing, I sent New York my own preballot assessment. I noted the widespread evidence of continuing TNI involvement in or support for the resurgence of militia violence and the security risk to local and international (especially Australian) UNAMET personnel. I said I believed that this was despite a Jakarta policy, including on the part of Wiranto, that there should be a peaceful outcome to the consultation. My senior Indonesian interlocutors had come to acknowledge privately that TNI elements were involved and were insisting that this would be addressed. However, I wrote, "We, and perhaps they, are beginning seriously to doubt their ability to control all TNI and militia elements."

When on 20 August I had the last of my many meetings with Zacky before Habibie ordered his withdrawal from East Timor, he had seemed to expect a rejection of autonomy. He raised concerns about the future of the 6,000 East Timorese members of the TNI, whom he saw as posing a risk of civil war. He estimated that more than 200,000 people, including family members, depended on Indonesian government salaries and suggested that help for them from the international community might lessen the possibility of violence. He said that the TNI would act to put a lid on violence to prevent itself from being blamed by the international community for an eruption of violence; and when I pressed him for action against the most threatening of the militia leaders, he said that the TNI had a special team to deal with them.

UNAMET's Foreign Ministry interlocutors, Zacky, police chief Silaen, and a number of other Indonesian officials gave the impression of expecting a pro-independence outcome. Thus, UNAMET's first concern was whether the ballot would be allowed to go ahead, and many of the reported plans and predictions were of violence to prevent it. It seemed that it would make little sense for the TNI to allow a pro-independence vote to take place and then react violently afterward, although some had doubts that the TNI would necessarily reason in that manner.

My assessment conveyed my own view and that of all senior UNAMET staff, supported by the CNRT and almost all diplomatic observers, that the ballot should go ahead, although we saw a possibility that it might be impossible to open polling on 30 August in some centers, subdistricts, or even districts. I strongly recommended contingency planning with key member states for two possible scenarios following the expected substantial majority for independence. The one I then considered most likely was that despite constructive intentions, the Indonesian authorities would be unable to prevent a flight of personnel and loss of morale leading to inaction by their security forces: the UN would be sucked into security and administrative functions, rather than being able to plan for an orderly transition. The other was that major violence might erupt during or after the ballot, with Indonesian security forces unable or unwilling to control the situation; they might concentrate on the extraction of their own personnel and tell the international community that the East Timor situation had become its problem, perhaps leaving behind arms for militia violence or encouraging destabilization from West Timor.

The Security Council received candid briefings on 24 and 26 August from Under-Secretary-General for Political Affairs Kieran Prendergast, reflecting UNAMET's latest reports of escalating violence and threats to its personnel. The Council issued strong statements after each briefing, and its president met the Indonesian Permanent Representative to express its concern. The Secretary-General issued his own statement and personally telephoned Habibie. The Core Group of countries that met in New York and Jakarta to discuss ways to support the UN's East Timor efforts—Australia, Japan, New Zealand, the United Kingdom, and the United States—acted both individually and jointly to impress upon Jakarta the international consequences if still worse violence were to occur. U.S. representations went from President Clinton to Habibie, Secretary of State Madeleine Albright to Alatas, and Secretary of Defense William Cohen to Wiranto. The Portuguese proposed that the Secretary-General should be in Dili with the Indonesian and Portuguese foreign ministers at the time the result was announced, but neither the UN nor Indonesia found this feasible. Prendergast suggested to the Security Council that it should send a mission of Council members prior to the announcement of the result to demonstrate the seriousness of its concern in the face of predictions of further violence, but the Council was not yet ready for such action. On 27 August, the Security Council met in formal session to adopt the resolution extending the mandate of UNAMET and increasing its uniformed strength, but no additional military or police would reach East Timor until after the vote.

On the eve of the ballot, UNAMET was bracing itself for the possibility of violence on polling day and the certainty of at least some violence to follow. Polling day would be better, and the aftermath far worse, than my expectations.

NOTES

1. *Report of the Secretary-General,* S/1999/862, 9 August 1999.

2. *Security Council Resolution 1262 (1999),* 27 August 1999.

3. Quoted in Commonwealth of Australia, Senate Foreign Affairs, Defence and Trade References Committee, *Final Report on the Inquiry into East Timor,* 7 December 2000, p. 183, footnote 161. Available online at http://www.aph.gov.au/senate/committee/fadt_ctte/East%20Timor.

4. See, for example, "Jakarta Plot to Reclaim Free Timor," *Sydney Morning Herald,* 20 July 1999.

5. For a careful analysis of the Garnadi document, see Geoffrey Robinson, "The Fruitless Search for a Smoking Gun: Tracing the Origins of Violence in East Timor," in Freek Colombijn and Thomas Lindblad, eds., *Violence in Indonesia: Its Historical Roots and Its Contemporary Manifestations* (Leiden: KITLV Press, forthcoming). Robinson concludes that "what it indicates most clearly is that, as of early July, contingency and operational planning for a pro-independence victory had not really begun. . . . [It] does not reveal anything like the degree of official involvement in planning of violence that some have claimed that it does." Robinson was a political affairs officer in UNAMET, responsible for the collation and analysis of its political reports from all districts.

6. Muis in *Sydney Morning Herald,* 24 August 1999, and *Jakarta Post,* 26 August 1999; Muladi in *Media Indonesia,* 27 August 1999.

7

Ballot and Revenge

PREPARATIONS FOR POLLING DAY

Amid all the violence and apprehension of the campaign period, UNAMET's electoral staff, the public information team, and the CIVPOL had been preparing themselves, the voters, and the Indonesian police for the ballot itself. The DEOs, having worked flat out for the continuous twenty-two days of registration, had had only the shortest of breaks before plunging into voter education throughout the villages. They were provided with cassettes, posters, banners, flyers, and leaflets produced by the public information and electoral teams in Dili. As well as ensuring that voters understood how to participate, the main messages, which were simultaneously being projected on television and radio, were aimed at minimizing the effects of intimidation. They included "your vote is secret"; "vote as you want, not as you are told"; "there will be one count in Dili"; "after the vote, UNAMET will stay"; and "peace is the prize." The UNAMET song, performed by a local group, and television skits using East Timorese actors were highly popular.[1]

The DEOs, while simultaneously having to attend to the exhibition of the voter lists, the recruitment and training of polling staff, and other preparations for the ballot, visited almost all villages in their areas of responsibility. In remote areas, they rented donkeys and rode them up into the hills to meet voters beyond the reach of vehicles. They addressed voters in the marketplace, at church congregations, and at cockfights, and they used role playing to explain the process. In Dili, electoral information was provided to the pro-autonomy and pro-independence parties, the church, and other civil society groups that could utilize their own distribution networks to disseminate it.

UNAMET, supported by the Electoral Commission, saw the decision that there would be one central count as important reassurance to communities that might fear reprisals, as it would ensure that there could be no knowledge of how individual districts or subdistricts had voted. In the run-up to the ballot, it became an issue of major contention with the pro-autonomy parties, who demanded that the votes should be counted locally. They argued that this was necessary for confidence that there would be no tampering. UNAMET met this with the assurance that Indonesian as well as UN police would accompany sealed ballot boxes at all times, including in UNAMET's helicopters, and the count itself would be fully open to observation. Some pro-autonomy leaders, including the governor of East Timor, had declared that if the overall vote was for independence, those districts with a pro-autonomy majority should nevertheless remain part of Indonesia. This suggested repartition of the island was lent plausibility by the assumption that the western districts, contiguous with West Timor, would be most likely to vote against independence. The demand for local counting was initially supported by the Indonesian Task Force, but they were overruled by Alatas; he at least was clearly alert to the dangers of encouraging talk of partitioning East Timor.

There was contention too regarding the accreditation of election observers. Since UNAMET was conducting the ballot, and was thus itself the object of observation, it obviously could not take on the role the UN has played elsewhere of coordinating the observers. It did, however, provide observers with accreditation and with an observer code of conduct. Nearly 2,300 observers were accredited. In addition to the 100 official Portuguese and Indonesian observers, around 490 international observers came from governments (Australia, Brazil, Canada, Chile, Ireland, New Zealand, and Spain, as well as the European Union) and nongovernmental groups (many of them Asian); and there were nearly 1,700 Indonesian and East Timorese nongovernmental observers. Many came from solidarity groups with a commitment to self-determination or independence for East Timor, but the observer code of conduct they accepted on accreditation required them to behave in a neutral manner. Ten days before the ballot, the official Indonesian observer delegation submitted applications for the accreditation of several hundred observers from some twenty-four Indonesian youth groups or other NGOs, transported to East Timor at government expense. They included groups that had been involved in political violence in Jakarta. CEO Fischer refused their accreditation on the grounds that they would create functional proxies for the official Indonesian observer delegation in violation of the terms of the agreements stipulating equal numbers.

When appealed to by the Indonesians, the Electoral Commission declined to intervene but pointed out that they could still witness the consultation process without the rights and obligations of accredited observers.

UNAMET was, however, conscious that the pro-autonomy side believed both that many of the observers were unsympathetic to it and also that UNAMET's local staff were largely pro-independence in their own sympathies. It therefore provided for party agents, which would have allowed UNIF and the CNRT to nominate representatives with access to polling stations and to the count. The CNRT had enough confidence in UNAMET to regard it as unnecessary to take up this offer. Less explicable was the fact that UNIF submitted no nominations before the deadline, set as late as was technically feasible; its only nominees were submitted from a single district, too late for accreditation to be possible, and included known militia members. They were still invited to nominate observers for the count. None of these facts would stop them from complaining about their alleged exclusion; already it seemed that they were preparing a case for challenging the outcome.

A key aspect of the planning for the ballot was the policing of polling day. UNAMET's police commissioner Mills worked closely and harmoniously with Indonesian police chief Silaen on their polling-day plans. There would be a single UNAMET CIVPOL officer at each of the 200 polling centers, whose responsibility to supervise the escort of ballot boxes was specified in the agreements. The Indonesian police would provide at least two armed officers for each center, an armed escort for the ballot boxes after the voting, and guards at the locations where ballot boxes would be held overnight. On the eve of the poll, Silaen's main concern was the possibility of attempts to hijack ballot boxes in transit if a pro-independence victory—which he now clearly expected—was evident. On polling day, while Marker would tour polling locations in one helicopter and I would remain at headquarters, Mills, Silaen, and Fischer would troubleshoot in another helicopter, and one helicopter would remain on standby for any medical or evacuation emergency.

EAST TIMOR VOTES

The DEO teams, with their CIVPOL colleagues, were in the field as early as 4:00 A.M. on Monday 30 August, moving materials and personnel into place and organizing their polling centers. They found large crowds of voters already waiting, and when reports came in from around the territory, UNAMET estimated that as many as 50 percent of all registered voters were present when polling began at 6:30 A.M. UNAMET and many observers had anticipated a high turnout, although the fresh displacement from recent violence and fear of what might follow cast some doubt on this; Maliana was a ghost town. But no one had expected such an overwhelming response. At every polling center, there were stories of the distances walked or other extraordinary efforts to vote by old, disabled, pregnant, or sick voters. Despite the early crowds, surprisingly few problems arose at the polling stations; voters stood quietly in queues for several hours under the burning sun, patiently waiting their turn. Most polling centers had processed nearly all their registered voters by 2:00 P.M., but they remained open until the official closing hour of 4:00 P.M. The count would show that fully 98.6 percent of all those registered had cast their votes.

Threatened militia violence, usually based on allegations against local staff at the polling stations, caused seven centers to suspend polling for some time. The Indonesian police cooperated well with UNAMET in enabling them all to reopen, and where necessary the voting hours were extended. The most serious violence was at Gleno, Ermera district, where around twenty militia arrived, shooting and throwing rocks and injuring two local staff; the situation was calmed and the center was the last to close, at 6:30 P.M. Meanwhile, as staff waited with ballot boxes at the close of the poll at a center in the distant Atsabe subdistrict of Ermera, a TNI officer and militia, all with automatic weapons, closed in on them, demanding that UNAMET's local staff members be handed over to them. The unarmed CIVPOL officer present was powerless to prevent an attack—in which polling staff were beaten, kicked, and stabbed. One of the victims was taken away by UNAMET staff after the attack and died of his stab wounds in a CIVPOL residence. Two others of the Atsabe staff would later be found to have been killed.[2]

The transport of the ballot boxes, to overnight collection points and then next morning to Dili, was in most places without serious incident, but the helicopter collecting the Maliana boxes was shot at, and there were tense and dangerous standoffs in Gleno and Atsabe. It took great courage on the part of international staff protecting both their local colleagues and the ballot boxes, the intervention of UNAMET's police commissioner, and some remarkable flying by the Australian helicopter crews before ballot boxes and local staff—more of whom would certainly have been killed had they been abandoned—were extracted to Dili.[3] At 6:00 A.M. on 31 August, the reconciliation of ballots began in the counting center, the Dili museum.

AWAITING THE RESULT

Marker and I met with international observer delegations before they began to disperse and found them uniformly positive about UNAMET's conduct of the ballot and deeply concerned about the security situation. The statement of the Irish foreign minister, as personal representative of the presidency of the European Union, was typical in paying tribute to "the professional, effective and dedicated way in which UNAMET staff conducted the poll."[4] In Jakarta, Alatas welcomed the fair conduct of the ballot and hoped that when the results became public none would claim that it was not free and fair. The government, he said, was watchful of some of the things done by certain individuals within UNAMET, but UNAMET as a whole should be congratulated for a job well done. Wiranto was quoted as saying that "on the whole" the UN had done a good job of supervising the ballot.[5]

A different view came from the pro-autonomy front, UNIF. From the morning of polling day, they voiced complaints of alleged irregularities, chiefly accusing UNAMET local staff of pressuring voters to mark their ballot papers for independence. As these complaints came in, CEO Fischer, the director of the UN's Electoral Assistance Division, Carina Perelli, and I went to polling centers concerned. We found that no such complaints had been made to the international staff overseeing them, and no irregularities had come to the attention of any of the election observers present. It was for the Electoral Commission, who had themselves been observing the polling process throughout the territory, to consider such complaints. The electoral commissioners announced that they would hold an open hearing, to which UNIF was invited to bring any witnesses to the alleged irregularities.

The hearing was held on 2 and 3 September. A series of mostly elderly witnesses were produced by the UNIF representative, claiming that they had been forced by UNAMET local staff to vote for "reject" when they had wanted to accept autonomy. After some of their evidence had been shown to be inconsistent or contradicted by observers, UNAMET's legal adviser submitted that there had been a preplanned strategy to call the integrity of the ballot into question by claiming bias and manufacturing complaints; in any event, even if every item of evidence that was presented on bias was accepted, it simply could not counter the overwhelming contrary evidence that the conduct of polling had been free and fair. The Electoral Commission concluded that "whatever merit there might be in individual complaints regarding alleged misconduct and/or partiality on the part of the electoral staff, none of them, singly or collectively, impaired the process as such."

UNAMET had been well aware of the need to protect against allegations of bias by limiting and supervising closely the role of local staff in the electoral process. Only international staff conducted the registration, and no local personnel were admitted to the count. For polling day itself, it was operationally imperative to utilize local staff, but this was done under the direct and constant supervision of international electoral officers. Impartiality and neutrality was the main message of all training. The regulations necessarily provided for assistance to voters physically unable to cast a ballot unaided. As far as possible, assistance was by international staff, but in some cases it had to be given by local staff. Whatever the sympathies of individual local staff, in a highly scrutinized ballot no objective observer reported any abuse of their position, and almost all praised the performance they witnessed.

Although the day-and-a-half-long Electoral Commission hearing was open to the media, amid the further violence that was breaking out it was little reported. The pro-autonomy critique had no shred of international credibility, but as it gained ground in the Jakarta media and political circles, Alatas and Wiranto urged that more be done to make known that the allegations had been taken seriously. Responding to this, the electoral commissioners went to Jakarta with the CEO, after the announcement of the result (and not before their own vehicle had been shot at in Dili), to give a press conference there on 6 September. This too received little coverage, and the Indonesian public remained unaware of the proper and lengthy procedures through which complaints had been considered.

It was evident that the pro-autonomy side had begun to understand from the overwhelming turnout that intimidation had failed, and their anger began to make itself felt even while the result was still awaited. The accusations against UNAMET local staff had further deadly consequences. On 1 September, hundreds of militia converged in Dili and attacked and burned houses of pro-independence supporters. There were killings outside the UNAMET compound, to which local people fled for refuge. Journalists were attacked and beaten; a BBC correspondent had his arm broken and was lucky to escape with his life. The next evening, militia surrounded UNAMET's regional office in Maliana, then went on the rampage, burning houses. Two UNAMET local staff were killed, and the international staff and those local staff still with them were withdrawn to Dili next day. Houses were burned in Liquiça, and the numbers of IDPs in the church compound at Suai and seeking refuge with Falintil were swelling.

When the Security Council heard an emergency briefing on 1 September, it issued a strong statement but was divided over Portugal's

plea that a Security Council mission should be in Dili for the announcement of the result. The following day, Marker met Alatas and Wiranto
in Jakarta to press yet again for effective action to control the militia,
whose activities continued unconstrained by the police or TNI; he
appealed to Wiranto to be in Dili for the announcement. UNAMET's
preballot hope that the East Timorese Consultative Commission would
exercise a calming influence proved futile. The FPDK nominees failed
to attend its 31 August inaugural meeting, save for one hard-liner whose
role was to block it from issuing even a brief call for reconciliation.
International scrutiny was shrinking fast. Many of the observers, some
of whom had themselves come under attack, were leaving. UNAMET
had accredited some 600 journalists, some of whom had always planned
to leave after polling day, but when the BBC chartered a plane to evacu-
ate its entire team, other journalists who had intended to stay for the
announcement left with them, despite the pleas of UNAMET's
spokesperson that they should remain. The departure of foreign
observers was clearly an objective of those directing the militia, but at
the same time, militia led by Eurico Guterres were occupying the Dili
airport terminal and screening passengers, with the openly declared purpose of preventing pro-independence and even some of the pro-autonomy leaders from fleeing.

Surprisingly, UNAMET's fears that the counting center might
become a target were not fulfilled, and the count proceeded according
to plan. UNAMET had been pressed to say when the result would be
announced. Apart from the time required for the count itself, it might be
necessary to allow time for the Electoral Commission to consider and
resolve any complaints and for the Secretary-General to interpret the
will of the people. A delayed result would feed suspicions. UNAMET
had therefore said, with due caution, that the result should be
announced "within seven days" of the ballot. But by 2 September, it
was apparent that the count could be completed during the night of 3–4
September, that the result would be overwhelming and require no inter-
pretation, and that the commission would be ready to give an immediate
determination. The growing insecurity argued for the earliest announcement of the result, which could in any case be expected to leak.

It had been agreed with the Indonesians that a morning announcement would best allow for any immediate reaction to be contained during daylight hours. I therefore informed the Indonesian Task Force that
the announcement would be made by the Secretary-General in New
York on the evening of 3 September, allowing the simultaneous
announcement to be made in Dili on the morning of 4 September. Muis
expressed dismay and asked for the announcement to be held back. This

could have been a concern in good faith to be better prepared to contain the situation. He had by then asked for Komando Strategis Angkatan Darat (Kostrad; Army Strategic Reserve Command) battalions to be sent to East Timor, and these troops were supposedly better disciplined than the territorial battalions and not contaminated by links with the militia. But the head of the Indonesian Task Force, with the concurrence of the police, agreed with UNAMET that the announcement should go ahead.

Few UNAMET staff slept during the night of 3–4 September. Additional hands were drafted to ensure that the count was completed. As soon as it had been, the Electoral Commission wrote their determination:

> The Commission was able to conclude that the popular consultation had been procedurally fair and in accordance with the New York Agreements, and consequently provided an accurate reflection of the will of the people of East Timor. There can be no doubt that the overwhelming majority of the people of this troubled land wish to separate from the Republic of Indonesia.[6]

At 9:00 A.M. on Saturday 4 September, as the Secretary-General made his announcement to the Security Council in New York, I read the same statement to the media in the Makhota Hotel in Dili; 21.5 percent had voted for autonomy and 78.5 percent had voted against. The Secretary-General called on the government of Indonesia to carry out its responsibility to maintain law and order in East Timor.

THE PUNISHMENT OF EAST TIMOR

The announcement was the signal for the outbreak of violence throughout East Timor. A first objective was to drive out foreign witnesses. In Dili, the remaining journalists and observers were immediate targets of intimidation. Outside Dili, the regional offices of UNAMET constituted the last international presence. Most electoral staff had already left the regions, as planned, but CIVPOL, MLOs, and security officers remained with a few other international staff. Some local staff had taken refuge with them; many others had already fled the towns and gone into hiding. By midday, just three hours after the announcement, an assault on the UNAMET compound in Liquiça began with numerous rounds of automatic weapons being fired at the front of the building. The UN staff drove at high speed out of the back of the compound toward the police station, their convoy coming under heavy fire from automatic and

homemade weapons, fired by militia, police, and at least one TNI sol-
dier. One vehicle had at least fifteen bullet holes, and bullets bounced
off a shovel held against the window of a vehicle by a female CIVPOL
officer. A U.S. CIVPOL officer, although wearing a bulletproof vest,
was hit twice in the stomach. He and the other staff were evacuated by
helicopter, and he was flown for medical treatment to Darwin, where
his injuries were treated successfully.

On the same day, staff withdrew amid outbreaks of violence from
Same, Ainaro, Aileu, and the Dili Regional Office. Militia were every-
where seen to be acting with the collusion of the TNI and police, who
were engaged in evacuating their own families to West Timor. Only in
Liquiça were UNAMET international staff attacked with clear intent to
kill, but elsewhere, amid threats and shooting, the police would advise
UNAMET that they could not guarantee their security and were with-
drawing. This clearly deliberate and coordinated pattern continued in
the next days. UNAMET was forced to withdraw from Suai and
Manatuto on 5 September, from Ermera and Viqueque on 6 September,
and from Baucau, Lospalos, and Oecusse on 7 September. In Baucau,
staff lay on the floor for two hours as Indonesian police fired automatic
weapons into the UNAMET office at chest height, before the TNI commander came to escort them to the airport.

In most places, the militia and their allies initially refused to allow
East Timorese staff to leave with UNAMET's road convoys or helicopters, but international staff consistently stood their ground, refusing to
leave without them. In Baucau, the international staff were flown
directly to Darwin. In the absence of Indonesian permission for the
local staff to leave East Timor (on which the Australian willingness to
fly them out depended), they were crammed onto grossly overcrowded
UNAMET helicopters and flown to join their colleagues in the Dili
headquarters compound. Throughout the evacuations, the helicopter
crews flew with great skill and courage in dangerous circumstances,
including being shot at. Once again, there can be no doubt that if local
staff had been left behind, many of them would have been killed.

As UNAMET withdrew to Dili, and its mobility and communications there became progressively restricted, its knowledge of what was
going on around the territory was limited. But already by 6 September,
UNAMET was reporting to New York, and telling world media in interviews from the compound, that there appeared to be a strategy to dis-
place large numbers of people and force them to move to West Timor.
There was widespread destruction of houses by burning and an
unknown number of killings. The pro-independence population, the target of the violence, had fled to the hills and forests and to places of

potential haven such as churches, the houses of nuns and priests, and the offices of UNAMET and the International Committee of the Red Cross (ICRC).

In Dili, the office of the Catholic diocese was attacked and burned on 5 September, and many people were killed there. On 6 September, the world was shocked by news of the destruction of Bishop Belo's house, when it and several other locations where IDPs were sheltering, including the ICRC compound, were attacked. Some were killed, but most were forcibly removed to the police headquarters and from there to West Timor. Bishop Belo was flown by Indonesian police to Baucau and left from there with the UNAMET evacuation to Darwin. The ICRC's expatriate staff were also forced to leave for Darwin. UNAMET had long feared an attack on the IDPs in the Suai church compound and had sought to gain them some protection through international attention to their situation. On 6 September, the three priests there were murdered and those they had been sheltering massacred. Only after the deployment of the peacekeepers would the scale of this and other massacres — at the Maliana police station on 8 September and in the enclave of Oecusse — become known, together with the toll of hundreds of individual killings and the prevalence of rape.[7]

It is for judicial proceedings to establish the responsibility of the planners and perpetrators of these crimes against humanity. Even at the time, it was evident to UNAMET that the relationship it had constantly observed and reported between the TNI and the TNI-created militia was operating more closely than ever. Indeed, some of the coerced East Timorese militia members had melted away, and much of the violence was directly perpetrated by TNI soldiers and by men in militia-style T-shirts identified as soldiers or not previously seen in the towns they were now destroying. The two territorial battalions of mainly East Timorese troops were acknowledged by Muis to be heavily involved; he described them as in mutiny. But the territorial battalions were commanded by Indonesian officers who were seen present at attacks, and a major role must have been played by the Kopassus special forces and Kopassus-trained commandos — sometimes disguised as police — whose presence was confirmed to UNAMET by Indonesian police officers. Police too participated in violence, although their major role was the implementation of the removals to West Timor.

Wiranto had not acceded to Marker's request that he be in Dili on the day of the announcement, but he, Alatas, and Muladi flew in (and out) the next day, 5 September. I met them at the airport and told them that UNAMET believed that the U.S. police officer seriously wounded the day before had been shot by a member of either the TNI or police.

The senior MLO from Maliana gave an eyewitness description of the involvement of the TNI in the violence there, led again by the commander who had supposedly been replaced. The Indonesians told UNAMET that the security forces were using persuasion to get the militia to stop the violence; if they were to shoot militia members, there would be war. Wiranto met with his commanders and with militia leaders. Only one CNRT leader who had not yet fled could be found to be present: José da Costa (Hodu Ran Kadalek, known as Mau Hodu), who had been working hard with the KPS to promote reconciliation. He would later be taken to West Timor, where he disappeared after being taken by militia from the hotel where he was staying with his family in Kupang.

The Indonesians expressed concern about the intentions of Falintil, which they repeatedly said had received new weapons—something never observed in the UN's contacts with them during or long after the consultation. The pressure on Falintil to take action was immense, as IDPs flocked to their cantonments with accounts of the violence from which they were fleeing. Gusmão stood firm in his orders that they were not to engage, and his relationships with his commanders as they spoke by satellite phone were tested almost to the limit. UNAMET's MLOs and political staff maintained phone contact with Falintil commanders they had come to know well, keeping them informed of the developments toward international intervention.

In Jakarta, the government stood firm in its opposition to the deployment of an international force. In meetings with Marker on 6 September, Habibie and Alatas angrily ruled out any suggestion that Indonesia should invite international assistance to arrest the murder and arson raging in East Timor. Habibie decreed the introduction of martial law from 7 September, the basis for another round of assurances to the international community that the situation was being brought under control. In East Timor, it made little difference: the violence and destruction continued unabated.

THE WITHDRAWAL OF UNAMET

From the day of the announcement, UNAMET staff in Dili were unable to sleep in their houses or hotel rooms, most of which were early candidates for looting and burning. They snatched the little sleep permitted by the shooting around them in their offices in the headquarters compound. Next to it was a school compound, which had become a place of refuge for IDPs. Just after nightfall on 5 September, sustained automatic

weapons firing close by caused the IDPs to panic; they hurled themselves and their babies over the razor wire that divided the compounds.
From then on, the UNAMET compound was home to some 1,500–2,000
IDPs, as well as the hundreds of local and international staff. Others
who found their way there included the Portuguese official observers,
whose house had been an early target of attack, and some twenty journalists who had courageously remained in Dili when their colleagues
left but had been forced out of their hotels.

Several UN vehicles had been shot at in the city, and it had become
impossible for UNAMET to move outside the compound without a TNI
escort; when it did, it was now without radio communication.
Automatic weapons fire around the compound was commonplace,
although most of it was shooting in the air by the police supposedly
protecting UNAMET. Only a couple of rounds entered the compound,
but the detonation of a grenade immediately outside was unsettling. On
7 September, the police were replaced by Kostrad troops, in whom
UNAMET hoped it could have somewhat greater confidence. But that
day—supposedly the first day of martial law, although the newly
appointed martial law commander had yet to arrive—UNAMET's vehicle workshop was destroyed and with it the satellite dish that provided
its main communications. Local telephones went out, as did the electricity and water supply. Fortunately, the compound—now a refugee
camp with impending health risks—had its own supply of well water,
but UNAMET became dependent on limited fuel stocks for its own gen-
erator. The helicopters were withdrawn, as insurance coverage became
impossible. The only other remaining international presence in Dili, the
Australian consulate, was in a similar position to UNAMET; surrounded by shooting and protected by Kostrad troops, its power and communications were failing. It was closed down and the consul and most staff
withdrawn on 8 September, although two military attachés stayed on to
liaise with UNAMET and the TNI and to facilitate whatever future
action the Australian Defence Forces might be required to undertake.

As Designated Official for Security, I was responsible for recommendations to New York regarding the security of UN personnel. On 8
September, after reviewing the situation with the senior military, police,
and security officers, I decided that I had to recommend a general evacuation. It was a decision reached with extreme reluctance, in view of
the commitment given to the East Timorese that UNAMET would stay
and because of the situation of the IDPs in the compound. Some days
before, I had asked the UN and the Australian government to make the
decisions necessary for local staff to be evacuated to Darwin; unusual
as this was, it was readily agreed to in New York and Canberra, and the

Secretary-General then personally obtained Indonesian consent from Habibie. But this did not extend to the IDPs in the compound; any commitments the Indonesians might make to the IDPs' safety after an evacuation of UNAMET would be of doubtful credibility.

Security "Phase Three," in UN parlance, had been declared on 4 September, implying the evacuation of "nonessential" staff. Many of those who had been intended to remain had been flown out to Darwin, as a return to the regions was inconceivable, movement out of the compound became impossible, and conditions inside deteriorated. By 8 September, some 192 international staff, CIVPOL, and MLOs remained. But CIVPOL and MLO contingents were questioning their continued presence, as were the authorities in several contributing countries. In weighing my decision, I was particularly swayed by information from inside the Korem Wiradharma 164 Dili (Komando Resort Militer; East Timor military headquarters). UNAMET's senior Australian MLO had been a staff college classmate when Muis undertook training in Australia. In the crisis, he had been posted to liaise with Muis and had been spending twenty-four hours a day inside the Korem. He never came to doubt the commander's intention to protect UNAMET's international personnel, but what he saw inside the Korem (before the level of threat to him required his withdrawal) led him to question whether this could in fact be guaranteed. The TNI had been engaged in destroying documents, apparently in preparation for their own departure. A final incident that morning, in which the senior security officer from New York participated, entered into the equation. With food and drinking water running short, a UNAMET team with TNI escort went to its warehouse at the port. Notwithstanding the TNI presence, they were surrounded by armed militia who pointed firearms at them, including to the head of a CIVPOL officer, and struck and damaged their vehicles. They returned empty-handed.

In New York, the Secretary-General, while deeply conscious of the strength of the political arguments for UNAMET to hang on, consistently respected the need to accept the judgment of the person on the ground. I was therefore authorized to proceed to negotiate evacuation arrangements with the Indonesian and Australian military representatives in Dili. As staff were informed of this, some were horrified at the prospect of leaving behind the IDPs and immediately volunteered to remain behind. Staff wept as they informed representatives of the IDPs that UNAMET might be departing the next morning; some of the young men left for the hills during the night. New York too suggested the possibility of volunteers remaining. I asked for a full list to be drawn up of those willing to volunteer to stay. I then went to the Korem to negotiate arrangements for the evacuation of international and local staff, and commitments regarding the safety of the IDPs with the TNI commanders: regional commander Damiri; martial law commander Major General Kiki Syahnakri, who had arrived that day but had not yet assumed command; and East Timor commander Muis.

The TNI commanders, who had to be relied upon to get those leaving to the airport in safety, wanted a predawn departure along a route to be heavily protected by Kostrad troops—a deployment that would not be possible before the following night of 9–10 September. During the meeting, Muis was called away to speak to Wiranto and returned with instructions to convey Wiranto's appeal that UNAMET should not leave, accompanied by renewed assurances of protection of the compound. The Security Council mission (described in the next chapter) had that day begun its meetings in Jakarta, where the government was trying to make the case that martial law was bringing the situation under control and international intervention was unnecessary. The mission and the Secretary-General, in his telephone discussions with Habibie, were impressing on the Indonesians the condemnation that would fall upon Indonesia if UNAMET had to pull out completely and if the IDPs were attacked. While I was at the Korem, the Security Council was receiving a morning briefing in New York. The Secretary-General told them that he hoped that some staff would stay, and the Council called on Indonesia to provide full protection for the East Timorese who had taken refuge in the UNAMET compound.

In the light of my discussions at the Korem, the evacuation was postponed for twenty-four hours, during which time the list of volunteers to stay was completed. It went ahead at dawn on 10 September. Some eighty international staff remained with the IDPs, including Police Commissioner Mills, CMLO Rezaq, and myself, while around 110 left with the local staff, and others who had been in the compound (including relatives of Ramos-Horta, and the Portuguese observer mission and their local staff), on Australian military planes to Darwin. The TNI mounted a professional operation to guard the route to the airport and escort the convoy. Syahnakri would later state that the plans for the 10 September evacuation had been passed to the militia, and four truckloads of Besi Merah Putih were intercepted in attempts to set an ambush for UNAMET.[8] But as I was at the airport to see that all the East Timorese evacuees were allowed to leave, the weakness of the TNI's undertakings to protect the compound was shown again. A group of militia armed with grenades as well as guns and machetes was allowed to penetrate the TNI cordon into the schoolyard next to UNAMET and up to its front gate, where unarmed UNAMET staff confronted them. Some of those who had stayed now favored immediate evacuation, believing that there was a serious threat that militia might come over the wall into the main compound and that the TNI would not provide meaningful resistance. On my return from the airport, where I had been out of communication, I concluded that we should remain. But while most of the volunteers were highly committed to staying until the future of the IDPs could be resolved, most believed it would then be right to leave.

The UNAMET volunteers hung on, and on 11 September we and the IDPs were visited by the Security Council mission. During that day, the momentum toward the Indonesian government's acceptance of international intervention became clear, and it was announced the next day. This, however, carried a further risk for UNAMET and the IDPs: that those TNI and militia still completing the destruction of East Timor would make them a target for their anger at the humiliation of international intervention before it arrived to protect us. UNAMET had immediately rejected the TNI's first proposal that the IDPs should be taken to police headquarters, from where they would at best have been transported, against their wishes, to West Timor. A possible alternative in which Muis agreed to cooperate was that they be escorted to join the pro-independence IDPs around Dare, in the hills above Dili, but this did not offer enough security en route or thereafter; those in Dare, with whom UNAMET was in communication, reported an extreme shortage of food and fear of attacks. The only fully secure option was their evacuation to Australia. Prime Minister Howard agreed to this, I pressed Wiranto on the issue when he came to Dili on 11 September, and the Security Council mission and ultimately the Secretary-General obtained Habibie's authorization. It remained for UNAMET and the Australian military representatives to negotiate the arrangements with the TNI. The IDPs and most of those who had stayed with them, including myself, left for the airport in another operation with well-organized TNI protection in the early hours of the morning of 14 September, and thence to Darwin. The UNAMET compound was closed, and a final brave group of twelve UN staff, headed by CMLO Rezaq, moved into the former Australian consulate, surrounded by Kostrad troops. There they awaited the arrival of international forces.

NOTES

1. See David Wimhurst, "The United Nations Information Intervention in East Timor," in Monroe E. Price and Mark Thompson, eds., *Forging Peace:*

International Intervention, Media and Conflict (Edinburgh: Edinburgh University Press, forthcoming).

2. First UN statements referred to one staff member killed in the Atsabe attack; the second death was confirmed soon after. With the two killings in Maliana, this brought known deaths of local staff to four. The third Atsabe killing was confirmed later. Other deaths or disappearances of local staff were reported after the UN's return. All are subject to investigation by the United Nations Transitional Administration in East Timor (UNTAET).

3. There is an account of these events, as told to the head of the Australian observer delegation, in Tim Fischer, *Seven Days in East Timor* (Crows Nest, NSW: Allen and Unwin, 2000), pp. 99–102.

4. Presidency of the European Union, *Statement on the Popular Consultation in East Timor by the Personal Representative of the Presidency Mr. David Andrews, Minister of Foreign Affairs of Ireland,* Dili, 31 August 1999. The appraisal of the head of the Australian observer delegation is contained in Fischer, *Seven Days in East Timor.* On the performance of UNAMET local staff, he writes: "Some local staff were overawed, especially at the beginning of polling day, but soon overcame their nervousness. There were one or two very minor irregularities, but these were quickly rectified. None of these irregularities could take away from the extraordinary overall efficiency, effectiveness and integrity of this very popular consultation" (p. 79).

5. *AFP*, "Indonesian Foreign Minister Says East Timor Vote Was Fair," 31 August 1999; *Sydney Morning Herald,* "Alatas Calls on Rivals to Accept Result," 1 September 1999.

6. Electoral Commission Determination, Dili, 4 September 1999. See Appendix 6.

7. Preliminary assessments are in the report on the joint mission to East Timor undertaken by the Special Rapporteur of the Commission on Human Rights on extrajudicial, summary or arbitrary executions, the Special Rapporteur on the question of torture, and the Special Rapporteur on violence against women, *Situation of Human Rights in East Timor,* A/54/660, 10 December 1999; *Report of the International Commission of Inquiry on East Timor,* A/54/726-S/2000/59, 31 January 2000; and Komnas HAM, *Report on the Investigation of Human Rights Violations in East Timor, Executive Summary,* Jakarta, 31 January 2000. Much more has become known as a result of investigations and exhumations by UNTAET, and will become public through judicial proceedings and the work of the East Timor Commission on Reception, Truth and Reconciliation.

8. Don Greenlees and Robert Garran, *East Timor* (Crows Nest, NSW: Allen and Unwin, forthcoming), chap. 9.

8

International Intervention

PREPARATIONS AND THE DIPLOMATIC CRESCENDO

The UN's formal planning beyond the ballot had been within the framework of the agreements and assumed that Indonesia would maintain responsibility for security throughout Phase II, advised by increased numbers of UNAMET CIVPOL and with an expanded military liaison presence. Only after Indonesia's MPR had acted on a pro-independence vote would the UN deploy a Phase III peacekeeping force. Obviously there had to be contingency planning for a worst-case scenario in which an extraction force might be necessary to pull out UNAMET and other foreign nationals. Australia had doubled its combat-ready troop strength, putting a second brigade on readiness, and had undertaken quiet planning to act unilaterally with the agreement of Indonesia should this be necessary; New Zealand too had placed troops on standby. Australia was also prepared to take the lead in the Phase III force, but it made clear throughout that any deployment of Australian troops to East Timor could take place only with Indonesian consent.[1]

As the scale of postballot violence and the role of the TNI became clear, those who had long been arguing for an international military presence in East Timor redoubled their appeals. Even before the result was announced, Portugal was calling for swift action to establish an international force if the situation deteriorated, and Australia recognized the likely need for accelerated deployment. The countries already on standby (Australia and New Zealand), and the permanent members of the Security Council most involved (the United Kingdom and the United States), discussed the possibilities with the Secretariat. One option might be to bring forward the deployment of the UN peacekeeping force that was being planned for Phase III, but acting within the full

UN procedures for mandating and assembling this would take weeks if not months. Even if a vanguard of the Phase III force could be deployed rapidly, it now appeared that its early task would be peace enforcement rather than peacekeeping. The discussions quickly concluded that the only effective means of rapid intervention would be a "coalition of the willing," mounted by a group of states under a Security Council mandate but outside UN procedures, pending the mobilization of a UN force ready to deploy into a more permissive environment. Already on 4 September, Australian foreign minister Alexander Downer spoke publicly of Australia's willingness to lead such a coalition, with Indonesian agreement and Security Council authorization. In his own statement that day celebrating the result of the ballot, Gusmão foresaw "a new genocide" and "total destruction" and called on the international community to save the people of East Timor with the immediate dispatch of an international force to impose peace.

The first diplomatic efforts continued to be aimed at inducing Indonesia to take effective action itself to end the violence in East Timor; member states varied in how quickly they reached the conclusion that this would not happen. The next objective was to obtain Indonesian agreement to international intervention. Neither Australia nor any other country would go in without it, or without authorization from the Security Council, where the support of China and Russia as well as of several nonpermanent members would itself depend on Indonesian acquiescence. No country suggested following the Kosovo precedent for unauthorized intervention, although sensitivity to the comparison or contrast with Kosovo may have intensified the diplomatic efforts of some governments. The third objective was to assemble a coalition of countries willing to take part, which would be militarily viable and as politically acceptable as could be achieved.

Secretary-General Annan and Prime Minister Howard, in continual contact with each other, took the lead in intense diplomatic efforts toward these objectives. On 5 September, after UNAMET's withdrawal from most regions had exposed the extent of the violence and had been reported to a Sunday briefing of the Security Council, the Secretary-General phoned Habibie. The president remained firmly opposed to any early deployment of international forces. But having had reports from Wiranto, Alatas, and Muladi on their visit to Dili, he was planning to declare martial law, and he opened the door to accepting international assistance if this failed to control the situation: "We will say the UN is coming in as a friend."[2] The Secretary-General added public pressure to his private persuasion by declaring when martial law was announced on

6 September that further measures would have to be considered if the situation did not improve within forty-eight hours.

A key initiative contributed to the dual purposes of persuading Indonesia and obtaining consensus in the Security Council. The Secretariat's proposal of a Security Council mission, first made on 26 August and discussed again at the urging of Portugal on 1 September, finally found general agreement when Under-Secretary-General Prendergast pressed it again on 5 September. Once the decision to mount the first such mission since 1994 had been made, it was fielded with impressive speed. It fell to the Netherlands presidency of the Council to determine the composition of the mission, and Ambassador Peter Van Walsum later explained how he did so:

> I invited the permanent representative of Namibia [Ambassador Martin Andjaba] to chair the mission because he was my predecessor, had done a very good job in that capacity and was African. As the other four members of the mission I selected the permanent representative of the United Kingdom [Ambassador Jeremy Greenstock] because his country had long played the leading role in the East Timor file, my Slovenian colleague [Ambassador Danilo Türk] on account of his expertise in international law, my Malaysian colleague [Ambassador Hasmy Agam] in view of his country's close ties with Indonesia and my deputy [Minister Alphons Hamer] because I wanted the presidency to be represented.[3]

The mission left New York on 6 September, accompanied by Deputy PRSG Vendrell, and reached Jakarta to begin its meetings on 8 September.

In its first meeting, the mission found Alatas firmly resistant to any foreign military presence before the MPR had acted on the consultation result. Next day, Habibie too stood firm; in the presence of his ministers, he was perhaps less ready to admit the possibility of international assistance than he had already been in private discussion with the Secretary-General. It is likely that he had needed to proceed first by way of martial law, and to allow Wiranto to be convinced that this was not enough, before he could give in to international intervention. Rumors of a coup to oust Habibie that were swirling around Jakarta were taken seriously by some in the diplomatic community. The mission sought to broaden the basis of eventual Indonesian acceptance of international assistance by meeting with Megawati Sukarnoputri, regarded then as Habibie's likely successor.

The mission's own determination grew as it heard briefings from UNAMET staff and the best-informed Jakarta embassies and received worsening news from East Timor, including the evacuation of most of UNAMET and the plight of the IDPs. Gusmão had at last been released on 7 September. In the midst of the violence sweeping East Timor, the Indonesians had initially insisted on releasing him in Dili and handing him over to UNAMET, who would then transfer him to Falintil's headquarters. Besieged in its own compound, UNAMET refused to accept this responsibility. Gusmão himself wanted to return immediately to East Timor, but Samuel and others persuaded him to consider temporary alternatives. In the end, he was released and handed over to UNAMET in Jakarta, to be transferred under heavy police escort to temporary accommodation in the British Embassy until arrangements could be made for him to travel to Darwin. In an emotional meeting with the mission, he appealed to them, as he did by telephone to the Secretary-General, to act immediately to save lives in East Timor. The mission insisted that it must fly to Dili to assess the situation at first hand and show support for UNAMET and must meet Habibie again on its return.[4]

Meanwhile, other pressures were growing. The nongovernmental East Timor solidarity network had become highly effective during the 1990s and worked closely with Ramos-Horta as the CNRT's main external spokesperson; it now went into overdrive. Human rights organizations called for action to check the violations and hold those responsible to account. The concern of the Catholic Church deepened as news came out of the killings of priests and of the attack on Bishop Belo's house; the pope spoke out, and Bishop Belo traveled to Rome and Lisbon. Media coverage was extraordinarily intense, with East Timor in the headlines and leading news bulletins for days. Television footage of violence and of desperate East Timorese scrambling over razor wire into the UNAMET compound was watched by a world still moved by the peaceful and dignified images of voters on polling day. The voices and reports of the small group of journalists who remained in Dili, and of UNAMET's staff speaking from the besieged compound and from Darwin, sustained the focus on the destruction, the forced displacement of the population, and the plight and responsibility of the UN. In Portugal, President Jorge Sampaio, Prime Minister Antonio Guterres, and Foreign Minister Jaime Gama worked the telephones twenty-four hours a day from the presidency. The whole country came to a halt on 8 September; Guterres himself participated in a human chain that snaked around the Lisbon embassies of permanent members of the Security Council, and there were vigils and demonstrations throughout the country demanding action. Australia was second only to Portugal in the extraordinary expressions of public opinion, and in Europe and elsewhere the response was strong.

Fortuitously, the Asia-Pacific Economic Cooperation (APEC) leaders' meeting was scheduled to take place in Auckland, New Zealand, with foreign ministers gathering on 9 September and heads of government on 12 September. APEC was strongly resistant to its agenda moving beyond strictly economic issues, but Canada proposed that there must be discussion of the East Timor crisis. New Zealand, as host country, was initially cautious, but amid enormous public concern and pressure from nongovernmental organizations was soon persuaded. It convened a Special Ministerial Meeting to discuss events in East Timor, alongside rather than as part of the APEC meeting itself. The UK was not an APEC member, but Foreign Secretary Robin Cook flew in to join the meeting with a European Union mandate, and Lloyd Axworthy of Canada, Don McKinnon of New Zealand, Madeleine Albright of the United States, Downer, and Cook met to coordinate strategy. Indonesia might have expected that its Asian allies would absent themselves from such a meeting, and the sponsors were at first uncertain to what extent the Asian countries would participate; the New Zealand liaison officers quietly lobbied the delegations. In the end, nearly all participated, and mostly at the level of their foreign minister or most senior representative present.[5] There was no collective statement, but the meeting served as a strong demonstration to Indonesia of the concern shared throughout its region. McKinnon as chairperson of the meeting summarized the consensus, and Cook spoke out strongly, pointing out that three-quarters of the world's GDP had been represented around the table, that the violence to frustrate the ballot was futile, and that the countries at the meeting were willing to support an international presence to help in ending it. Habibie and Alatas, who were to have represented Indonesia, had cancelled their attendance, but the senior Indonesian economic minister as well as McKinnon conveyed the message back to Jakarta.[6]

The economic minister had good reason for concern, stemming from even more crucial quarters. Since the rupiah had slumped amid the Asian economic crisis, Indonesia had become more dependent than ever on the International Monetary Fund (IMF) and the World Bank. East Timor had featured at the Paris meeting of the Consultative Group for Indonesia (CGI) convened by the World Bank in late July 1999, when donors' pledges were put in the context of support for Indonesia's political transition, including "the Government's commitment to provide the security necessary for the August popular consultation on East Timor." At that meeting, the government had declared that it was "determined to implement our part of the agreement, and give our full support to the operations of the United Nations in East Timor." This provided a basis for the Bank to respond to the postballot violence by issuing what was perhaps its strongest-ever public statement regarding a political situation, referring to East Timor as "of paramount concern to our shareholders." Bank president James Wolfensohn wrote to Habibie on 8 September, stating that CGI donors had based their commitments on the assurances given in July: "For the international financial community to be able to continue its full support, it is critical that you act swiftly to restore order, and that your government carry through on its public commitment to honor the referendum outcome."[7] The IMF issued successive statements that it was closely watching the situation in East Timor and on 9 September announced that it was putting on hold a planned mission to Indonesia on which the resumption of IMF lending depended.

The economic consequences for Indonesia were not immediate; lending had already been suspended as a result of financial scandal at Bank Bali. But each of the statements, by institutions historically inclined to confine themselves to strictly economic criteria and reluctant to take account of political situations, was almost unprecedented; together they were a heavy warning of Indonesia's potential isolation and the eventual economic consequences. This was not the result of U.S. pressure; although they must have been aware of the wishes of donor countries, the respective presidents (Wolfensohn of the Bank and Michel Camdessus of the IMF) must be credited with their strong responses to the destruction of East Timor.[8]

The U.S. government was, however, now ratcheting up its own pressure. Its first response to the postballot violence was to intensify the representations it had already been making for the TNI to control the situation: Clinton to Habibie, Albright to Alatas, the chairman of the joint chiefs of staff to Wiranto. The commander in chief of the Pacific Command flew to Jakarta to deliver a face-to-face message to Wiranto on 9 September. But the ability of the United States to send a strong signal on the need for international intervention was initially constrained by its limited willingness to participate in it.

From 4 September, officials in Washington were examining what involvement in an Australian-led coalition they could recommend. The NGO lobby on East Timor in the United States had been highly effective over the years and now worked with its friends in Congress to put pressure on the administration. On 6 September, Albright, then in Hanoi, said that Indonesia would have to let the international community deal with the situation if they did not stop the violence themselves. Australia, which wanted not just U.S. support in the Security Council but U.S. participation in the military coalition, applied its own pressure, not only through Howard's telephone persuasion of Clinton, but publicly too. In a series of interviews on 7 September, Downer spoke of the Pentagon's reluctance and voiced Australia's feeling that the United

States should reciprocate the contributions Australia had made as a U.S. military ally, most recently in the Gulf conflict with Iraq. Portugal was making similar claims of Clinton: how could Portugal send troops to Kosovo if there was not an equivalent international response to parallel crimes in East Timor? On 8 September, Australia was promised some U.S. military participation, although statements implying the contrary continued to come from Defense Secretary William Cohen and National Security Adviser Sandy Berger. At first, only logistical support was envisaged, but this was extended to a small number of military who would assume key noncombat roles on the ground in East Timor. The public message to Indonesia became clear when Clinton gave a press conference as he departed on 9 September for the APEC meeting: if Indonesia did not end the violence, it must invite — "it *must* invite," he repeated emphatically — the international community to assist in restoring security. He threatened economic sanctions through the international financial institutions and announced the suspension of all programs of cooperation with the Indonesian military. He did not yet cut off commercial arms sales to Indonesia; that came two days later as he arrived in Auckland and further toughened his statements. Also on 11 September, the UK suspended sales of Hawk fighter jets to Indonesia, and the European Union concluded agreement on its own arms boycott on 13 September. The weight of international pressure building up on Jakarta was well illustrated by the banner headline of the *Washington Post* of 10 September: "US, IMF move to isolate Jakarta; Clinton cuts ties to Indonesia military; loan program suspended."

Asian pressure was of a different style, but significant. Japan was a member of the Core Group, coordinating diplomatic efforts in New York and Jakarta with Australia, New Zealand, the United Kingdom, the United States, and the UN Secretariat. It followed the security situation in East Timor closely. Its sending of senior CIVPOL officers to UNAMET had been something of a psychological breakthrough for Tokyo, where it had been closely debated. Japan had been traumatized by the killing of a Japanese policeman in Cambodia in 1993, since when it had not been willing to send police officers to UN missions. Japan's warnings to Habibie before and after the ballot were conveyed privately, and no doubt in its own style, but insistently; they carried the weight of Indonesia's leading investor and trading partner.

On 10 September, the Secretary-General made his strongest statement yet. Announcing that Australia, New Zealand, the Philippines, and Malaysia had indicated willingness to participate in an international force, he urged the Indonesian government to accept their offer of help without delay: "If it refuses to do so, it cannot escape responsibility for what could amount, according to reports reaching us, to crimes against humanity."[9] The UN High Commissioner for Human Rights, Mary Robinson, flew to Darwin, where she heard the accounts of those evacuated from East Timor and began to talk publicly of the need to bring to justice those responsible for such crimes.

In New York, the Security Council was being briefed daily in informal consultations but had not discussed East Timor in formal, public session since before the ballot. Portugal had requested such a session and was joined by Brazil. The Council President consulted Council members; the general view was that it would be illogical to dispatch a mission consisting of one-third of its members and not wait for them to return and report. He consulted the mission itself and found them of the same view. But personally convinced that public opinion would not understand if another weekend went by without the Council addressing itself to what was going on in East Timor, the President decided to act on his own authority. He called an open meeting for Saturday 11 September.[10]

Before the Council met, the members of its mission had been in East Timor viewing the destruction of Dili and UNAMET's compound, which had become an IDP camp. The day before their visit, 10 September, they had met Wiranto, surrounded by his generals at TNI headquarters in Jakarta. The mission leader, Andjaba of Namibia, had been forceful in stating that events on the ground made it clear that the Indonesian authorities were either unable or unwilling to meet their security responsibilities and must therefore accept the offer of international assistance. Wiranto once again rejected this, arguing that the TNI were best able to handle the situation. While the meeting was going on, staff in the UNAMET compound phoned through to a colleague accompanying the mission the news that militia had been allowed to penetrate the TNI cordon and were threatening UNAMET. Wiranto phoned Dili and assured the mission that this was an example of false information: the situation was peaceful. A second call from the compound confirmed that, on the contrary, the incident (described in the previous chapter) was continuing. Despite his efforts to minimize its significance, Wiranto was deeply embarrassed by the direct evidence of the failure of his soldiers—the elite Kostrad troops at that—to provide the security promised to UNAMET. The mission insisted that Wiranto himself should go to Dili with them.

Next morning, Wiranto flew to Dili ahead of the mission. He left Jakarta earlier than scheduled, leaving behind the group of journalists promised seats on his plane. Only those journalists for whom there was room on the TNI plane carrying the mission itself were able to provide

the world with the images and description of the destruction of the preceding week. Dili was quiet—another apparent indication of the ability
of the TNI to maintain a degree of calm when they chose to do so. But
nothing could conceal the extent of destruction or the misery of people
waiting at the police station and the port before being taken to West
Timor. At TNI headquarters, a slide presentation gave statistics of buildings burned that defied the evidence of even a cursory tour of the city.
The mission was briefed by those who had stayed on at UNAMET's
headquarters and was visibly moved as it talked to the IDPs and was
shown one of the babies delivered by UNAMET's doctor since the siege
began.

In the course of that day, Wiranto gave the first indications to the
mission—and to CNN—that he was considering a change of position
regarding international assistance. Members of the mission were convinced that he had been personally shocked by his visit to Dili. The mission left for Jakarta, now optimistic about a positive outcome to their
meeting with Habibie the next day.

As they arrived back in Jakarta, the open session of the Security
Council began in New York. The Secretary-General in his opening
statement reiterated that what was happening in East Timor might well
fall into various categories of international crime. He urged Indonesia to
agree without further delay to the deployment of an international force:

> The international community is asking for Indonesia's consent to the
> deployment of such a force. But I hope it is clear Mr. President that it
> does so out of deference to Indonesia's position as a respected mem-
> ber of the community of states. Regrettably, that position is now being
> placed in jeopardy by the tragedy that has engulfed the people of East
> Timor.

In a session lasting nearly six hours, no less than fifty delegations took
the floor—a highly unusual total—including some who rarely spoke as
nonmembers. Most condemned the violence in East Timor in the
strongest terms—not only the Portuguese-speaking and Western countries, but Latin Americans and others too. A majority of Security
Council members pressed strongly the need for Indonesia to accept an
international force; China and Russia stressed the need for Indonesian
consent and Security Council authority. Only a few of the countries of
the nonaligned movement displayed more concern about precedents for
intervention than about the situation in East Timor or supported
Indonesia's contention that it was capable of bringing the situation
under control. Asian countries expressed the need for understanding and
encouragement during Indonesia's political transition, but the Republic

of Korea and the Philippines hoped for Indonesia's agreement to international assistance and indicated willingness to participate. Overall, the session was a powerful demonstration of international outrage and Indonesia's growing isolation.

The session ended as the new day, 12 September, dawned in Jakarta. Habibie met with his cabinet. His promised meeting with the Security Council mission was held back until after the cabinet meeting to avoid further impression of conceding to pressure, but the mission knew they could relax. When the delayed meeting took place, Habibie informed them that he had telephoned the Secretary-General to call for UN assistance to restore peace and security in East Timor. He had known, he said, when he met them three days before that it could not be avoided, but he had needed Wiranto to visit Dili. The decision was, he said, without conditions: Alatas would fly to New York to work out the implementation. Habibie made his announcement to the Indonesian nation on television and radio—a calamitous eight days after the result of the ballot had been announced.

MANDATING INTERFET

Indonesia's request made it certain that the Security Council would mandate a force, and Alatas reiterated on his arrival in New York that he came without conditions. But Indonesia was in fact strongly opposed to Australian leadership of an international force, and there were several issues that had to be addressed before a resolution could be adopted.

Indonesia was highly sensitive to the role of Australia. It was clear that Australia would provide the core of the force, but Indonesia wanted as much Asian participation as possible and a force commander from the Association of Southeast Asian Nations. Australia was concerned about the immediate cooperation with Indonesia necessary for an effective military operation and about its long-term relationship with its largest neighbor. It had always made clear that it would act only with Indonesian consent and sought to ensure that the language of the Security Council resolution made it possible for Indonesia to accept the help of friends, rather than have to submit to demands.[11] But Australia regarded it as essential that it should command the force to which it would make the major contribution and that the force have a robust mandate.

Among Council members, Canada in particular would have preferred to see a force that was from the outset a UN force with blue berets, symbolizing UN authority and control, and that would stay on with the necessary adjustments into Phase III, rather than an initial multinational force replaced by a UN peacekeeping operation. UN procedures and the U.S. requirement to consult Congress meant that this was not compatible with the speed demanded by the situation and with which Australia was ready to move if authorized. The possibility was raised of a multinational force authorized by the Security Council wearing blue UN berets, but it was felt that this had to be reserved to a force under UN command. It was therefore agreed that the initial force would be a multinational force but that it would be replaced as soon as possible by a UN force, in which some of the same troops would come under UN command and don blue berets. Of the precedents for this, the closest was Haiti in 1994–1995.

The Secretary-General informed Indonesia that he was asking Australia to command the force, although the command might change for Phase III. He and Howard had, however, been working to maximize Asian participation. APEC leaders were still together in Auckland when it became clear that Indonesia would consent, and this provided a timely opportunity for discussions in the margins of the meeting about participation in the force. Thailand agreed to provide the deputy force commander along with its contingent. Malaysia scaled down its willingness to participate when the post of deputy force commander went elsewhere, but the Philippines and the Republic of Korea confirmed their commitments; Singapore too would send a medical company. New Zealand had long had a battalion on standby. The commitment of the United States and the United Kingdom, as permanent members of the Security Council with strong ties to Indonesia, was important; although small in numbers, their contributions were militarily as well as politically significant. The United States would provide only noncombat personnel, but its 385 personnel in East Timor provided what the force commander called "niche capabilities," including communications, intelligence, and civil affairs. Beyond this, 1,000 U.S. marines were stationed offshore, and the United States provided and absorbed the cost of the "lift" for other participants. The British Gurkhas, the first troops to go in with Australia and New Zealand, enhanced the force's immediate readiness for combat. Portugal was willing to send up to 1,000 troops but accepted the judgment that their major participation would better await Phase III.[12]

The UK had taken the lead in drafting Security Council resolutions and statements on East Timor, and other members pay tribute to the skill with which it did so. Australia and the United States were firm that the mandate must be a fully robust one under Chapter VII of the Charter. Indonesia's friends initially resisted this, preferring a weaker Chapter VI mandate, but Alatas himself had said that the role was peace enforcement, not peacekeeping, and accepted action under Chapter VII. The resolution therefore

> *authorizes* the establishment of a multinational force under a unified command structure, pursuant to the request of the Government of Indonesia conveyed to the Secretary-General on 12 September 1999, with the following tasks: to restore peace and security in East Timor, to protect and support UNAMET in carrying out its tasks and, within force capabilities, to facilitate humanitarian assistance operations, and *authorizes* the States participating in the multinational force to take all necessary measures to fulfil this mandate.[13]

The practice that the countries participating in such a multinational force have to themselves bear the costs of participation was a potential limitation on broadening the participation. The resolution therefore established a trust fund, which enabled countries that supported but did not participate in the operation to contribute to the costs of others. The major contributor was Japan.

Indonesia was still regarded as responsible for security in East Timor until the start of the implementation of the result of the ballot; the resolution looked forward to "close coordination between the multi-national force and the Government of Indonesia." Indonesia sent senior TNI representatives to New York, and they agreed to the UN and Australian arrangements for a joint consultative security group to ensure this coordination in Dili, comprising the force commander of the multinational force, the TNI commander and the chief of Indonesian police in East Timor, and UNAMET's CMLO and police commissioner.

The Security Council adopted the resolution on 15 September. Australia had placed its troops on formal alert on 8 September, to be ready either to extract UNAMET or to lead in a multilateral force. The leading elements of the force gathered in Darwin, and on 19 September, its Australian commander, Major General Peter Cosgrove, flew to Dili with his Thai deputy and other heads of national contingents. I accompanied him, in order to symbolize the close relationship between UNAMET and the force mandated to enable it to resume its functions. Cosgrove informed TNI commander Syahnakri of the landings planned for the following day, and on 20 September the International Force for East Timor (INTERFET) established its presence in Dili.[14]

FROM UNAMET TO UNTAET

The tired remnants of UNAMET, now at last being reinforced by the fresh MLOs and CIVPOL planned for Phase II, redeployed from

Darwin to East Timor as rapidly as security and some minimal arrangements for sleeping and eating amid the devastation permitted. First to move out from Dili were the MLOs, whose preexisting knowledge of the regions was invaluable to INTERFET and to the huge humanitarian operation that was getting under way, coordinated by the UN's Office for the Coordination of Humanitarian Affairs (OCHA). They were followed by CIVPOL and by the UNVs who had stayed on to be converted from electoral to civil affairs officers. They began to work with local CNRT leaders to address the most immediate needs. With the withdrawal of Indonesian and many East Timorese government officers and the destruction of buildings, all administration and most services had collapsed.

At a tripartite meeting with Portugal and the UN on 28 September, Indonesia agreed that although in its own eyes it maintained its de jure control of East Timor until its MPR determined otherwise, the UN could exercise de facto powers in the vacuum that existed. But UNAMET, staffed chiefly as an electoral mission, had none of the civilian personnel required for the administrative responsibilities that would now fall to the UN. Nor did it have investigative personnel, beyond a small number of hard-pressed CIVPOL, for the huge task of exhuming bodies and investigating the human rights crimes that had been perpetrated. This task was urgent; on 27 September, the Commission on Human Rights called on the Secretary-General to establish an international commission of inquiry to conduct an initial investigation into violations of human rights and humanitarian law in East Timor since January 1999. New personnel were painfully slow to arrive; indeed only a few police and no other civilians arrived until late October. On 4 October, the Secretariat published its proposals for the United Nations Transitional Administration in East Timor (UNTAET).[15] On 19 October, the MPR in Jakarta adopted its decision that the integration of East Timor within Indonesia was no longer applicable, although not before a serious attempt by some to make this conditional on further investigation of complaints that UNAMET had rigged the ballot. On 25 October, the Security Council mandated UNTAET, which incorporated the remaining staff of UNAMET.[16] On 22 October, Xanana Gusmão had received an emotional welcome on his return to East Timor, and on 30 October, the last Indonesian representatives departed.

The task ahead in East Timor was a daunting one for the East Timorese leadership and for the UN. It was made still greater by the forced displacement carried out alongside the destruction and killing. In New York, in order to take part in the first meetings between Gusmão and the Secretariat, I had briefed the Security Council on 1 October. Referring to UNAMET's consistent reporting, throughout the consultation period, on the activities of the militia and their TNI supporters, I said:

> I have chosen to focus here on the role of the militias and their link-ages not simply to repeat the analysis others have presented but because I believe the phenomenon has now been exported to West Timor, and as such may well continue to have an effect on the work of the UN in East Timor. East Timorese militias are now allowed to maintain themselves and a large element of control over refugee popu-lations in West Timor. A united front of East Timorese "integration fighters" has been declared. These developments beyond the borders of East Timor point towards a worrying conclusion that the militias may well continue to enjoy similar types of support now as they evi-dently did before. . . . The right of the refugees to return to East Timor must be strictly protected, especially given the forced deportation into exile which many of them have suffered.

Over a year later, this aspect of the international community's responsi-bility had cost further lives of UN staff—this time international human-itarian workers murdered by militia in Atambua—and still remained unfulfilled.

NOTES

1. On Australia's military planning, see Don Greenlees and Robert Garran, *East Timor* (Crows Nest, NSW: Allen and Unwin, forthcoming), chap. 10.

2. For an account of the Secretary-General's telephone diplomacy over this period, see William Shawcross, *Deliver Us From Evil* (New York: Simon and Schuster, 2000), pp. 390–397.

3. Peter Van Walsum, Ambassador and Permanent Representative of the Netherlands to the UN, speech, "The Netherlands Presidency and the East Timor Crisis," University Club, New York, 17 November 2000.

4. The mission's meetings are summarized in *Report of the Security Council Mission to Jakarta and Dili, 8 to 12 September 1999,* S/1999/976, 14 September 1999. More atmospheric accounts of the meetings can be found in a series of articles in the (London) *Independent,* 9–13 September 1999, by David Usborne, a journalist who accompanied the mission.

5. Ministers from Australia, Canada, Chile, Japan, Korea, Mexico, New Zealand, Peru, the Philippines, Singapore, Thailand, the United Kingdom, and the United States; senior officials from Brunei Darusalam, Malaysia, Papua New Guinea, the People's Republic of China, Russia, and Vietnam, as well as from Indonesia itself; media briefing, Auckland, 9 September 1999.

6. Indonesia's senior representative present was Ginandjar Kartasasmita, coordinating minister for economy, finance, and industry.

7. World Bank press release, "Donors Confirm Support for Indonesia,"

Paris, 28 July 1999; "World Bank Statement on East Timor," Washington, 7 September 1999.

8. Interviews with World Bank, IMF, and U.S. Treasury officials.

9. Secretary-General Kofi Annan, Statement on East Timor, New York, 10 September 1999.

10. Van Walsum, "The Netherlands Presidency and the East Timor Crisis."

11. On Australia's objectives and diplomacy during this period, see Alexander Downer, "East Timor: Looking Back on 1999," in *Australian Journal of International Affairs* 54, no. 1 (2000); and Penny Wensley, Ambassador and Permanent Representative of Australia to the UN, speech, "East Timor and the United Nations," Sydney, 23 February 2000.

12. On Australia's efforts to assemble the INTERFET coalition, see Greenlees and Garran, *East Timor,* chap. 10. Twenty-two countries ultimately participated in INTERFET: Australia (5,592 troops), Brazil (51), Canada (736), Denmark (2), Egypt (71), Fiji (189), France (643), Germany (81), Ireland (43), Italy (560), Jordan (707), Kenya (240), Malaysia (30), New Zealand (1,190), Norway (6), the Philippines (604), Portugal (285), the Republic of Korea (436), Singapore (275), Thailand (1,748), the United Kingdom (335), and the United States (639).

13. *Security Council Resolution 1264 (1999),* 15 September 1999. See Appendix 5.

14. On the deployment and early actions of INTERFET, see Greenlees and Garran, *East Timor,* chap. 11.

15. *Report of the Secretary-General on the Situation in East Timor,* S/1999/1024, 4 October 1999.

16. *Security Council Resolution 1272 (1999),* 25 October 1999.

9

Conclusion

THE INTERNATIONAL CONTEXT

The question of East Timor had been a highly particular one on the UN agenda since 1975, and the moment at which it came to center stage was initially determined by internal developments in Indonesia. However, the international response was influenced by the context of world affairs as it had come to be in mid-1999, although not necessarily in the way that is sometimes assumed.

As the 5 May Agreements were signed, NATO warplanes were bombing Serbia and Kosovo. Retrospective accounts of 1999 would bracket together Kosovo and East Timor as cases of "international humanitarian intervention." In fact, similarities are hard to find, and it is the contrasts that are instructive.

The international diplomacy regarding the impending Kosovo crisis was undertaken by an array of U.S., European, and Russian negotiators acting inside and outside a variety of international organizations: NATO, the European Union, the Organization for Security and Cooperation in Europe (OSCE), and only occasionally the UN. In the case of East Timor, diplomacy was UN-led, and the supportive efforts of the governments with the greatest interest and influence were coordinated effectively within a UN framework.

When it came to intervention in Kosovo, international law and national sovereignty were ultimately overridden. International action regarding East Timor, on the other hand, was taken with the full legitimacy of Security Council authorization. And even in a case where national sovereignty did not apply, since the UN did not recognize Indonesia's claim to sovereignty over East Timor, the Security Council was solicitous of the need for Indonesia's consent to intervention.

119

The Kosovo intervention left the status of the territory unresolved and the international community, including the Security Council, bitterly divided. Thus, when the UN inherited responsibility for a situation in Kosovo that was not of the UN's own making, it found itself handicapped by continuing uncertainty and divisions. The challenge of UN transitional administration in East Timor would, for all its difficulties, benefit from united international support toward the clear objective of independence.

Since East Timor came back onto the agenda of the Security Council when the agreements had been reached, giving effect to a popular consultation that was the proposal of Indonesia's president, there was initially no reason why it should trouble even the most reluctant interventionists among Council members. The first issue the Council faced was how to respond to the Secretariat's briefings, based on UNAMET's reporting, regarding the security situation. It repeatedly expressed concern in presidential statements and in meetings between the Council President and Indonesia's Permanent Representative. But the UK's draft statements, which reflected the information of Australia and the United States as well as the concerns of the Secretariat, often had to be softened to secure the support of Indonesia's friends on the Council, among whom Malaysia was the most influential and Bahrain the most uncompromising. As a traditional leader of the Nonaligned Movement, Indonesia commanded support among members of the G-77, who were predisposed to accept that Jakarta was doing its best to contain violence. Sympathy for Indonesia as a state undergoing a difficult transition to democracy was not, of course, confined to the G-77; U.S., Australian, European Union, and other policymakers were continuously conscious of the larger interest of a stable, democratic Indonesia.

As the issue within the Security Council moved on to the response to the postballot violence, and became one of possible intervention, the positions shaped by the recent Kosovo debate came into play. China and Russia, as well as the G-77, were insistent that international "assistance" should be only on the invitation of Indonesia. But this was not a matter of dispute, since the country willing to lead the intervention, Australia, itself preconditioned its willingness on Indonesian consent. Conversely, behind China and Russia's general position on intervention there was no special desire to protect Indonesia. Ethnic Chinese had been among the first victims of Indonesia's 1975 invasion of East Timor and had more recently been the target of racial killings and assault in Jakarta. Partially offsetting Indonesia's support among the G-77 was the solidarity of the Lusophone group with East Timor, while Portugal was constantly lobbying its European Union partners to take a robust stand.

However different the two situations, intervention in Kosovo would have made a failure to intervene in East Timor all the more impossible to defend, and decisionmakers had been repeatedly reminded of the shame heaped upon the UN for standing by at the massacres in Rwanda and at Srebrenica. No one was more conscious of this than Secretary-General Annan, whose personal human rights commitment led him to be more willing to advocate humanitarian intervention than the governments of most member states.

A FLAWED AGREEMENT?

At his news briefing on 10 September, where he appealed for collective pressure on Indonesia to accept international assistance to end the violence in East Timor, the Secretary-General was asked by a correspondent whether, looking back, anything could have been done to create a different outcome. Annan recognized that there were people who, in hindsight, were saying that the UN should not have accepted the word of the Indonesians that they would maintain law and order. But, he said, if that had not been accepted, there probably would have been no vote:

> We knew it was going to be difficult, we knew about the security problems, but not the carnage and the chaos we have seen. I can assure you that if those who were putting together the deal—and we must remember the agreement was signed by Portugal and Indonesia with the support of their leaders, unanimously endorsed by the [Security] Council—if any of us had an inkling that it was going to be this chaotic I don't think anyone would have gone forward. We are no fools.[1]

Some critics of Australian policy have argued that too much pressure was applied to a vulnerable Indonesia in late 1998, pushing a weak interim president into a high-risk decision to bring a hasty end to the East Timor issue, from which—even after he had made it—he should have been restrained. Others argue that much more pressure should have been applied to induce Indonesia to accept an international force in East Timor to maintain security for the ballot and beyond.

Even with the benefit of hindsight, neither argument is convincing. It was the political forces released in East Timor by change in Indonesia that led each of the actors—the UN, Australia, and ultimately Habibie—to perceive, correctly, that autonomy without self-determination would not settle the question of East Timor. The responsibility for deciding that the choice between autonomy and independence could only be an immediate one must rest with Habibie. He rejected the period of transition favored by the international community and East Timorese leaders, although perhaps this would in any event have proved not to be feasible. Once Habibie had offered that choice, the UN and the key countries following closely the UN's negotiations were well aware of the risk. But neither they nor the East Timorese could have countenanced the opposite risk—of failing to grasp an opportunity that had been closed for twenty-four years.

It was then the responsibility of the UN and Portugal to gain the best agreements, including the strongest security guarantees, they could, and of those with influence with Indonesia to support them in this. The security agreement fell well short of the UN's proposals for disarming the militia and neutralizing the TNI, and the UN's proposals themselves never envisaged a peacekeeping force before the ballot. Perhaps more could have been obtained at the negotiating table if Portugal and the UN had been willing to risk the very prospect of the agreement that they—and the CNRT—so strongly desired and had called for more U.S. and other pressure on Jakarta. But it is impossible to believe that this could have gone as far as inducing acceptance of an international peacekeeping force; Habibie could not have accepted this and survived politically to see it implemented. And only the presence of international peacekeepers with a robust mandate and the withdrawal of most of the TNI would have prevented the violence before and after the ballot. Further Indonesian security commitments short of this would have meant as little in practice as those that were given and dishonored.

The dishonoring of those commitments did not appear as inevitable at the time as it now appears in retrospect, although those—including the many East Timorese—who always expected a violent outcome proved to be right. Alatas was persuasive when he repeatedly pointed out that the offer of the two options was made by the Indonesian government, and it was not in its interest to see it collapse into violence. Australia and the United States believed that Wiranto represented a new leadership of the TNI, increasingly open to positive influence in a changing Indonesia. The optimists felt vindicated when predictions of violence in Indonesia's freest election in June 1999 were not borne out, and the security forces were judged to have acquitted themselves well. The risk was known, but it was not taken lightly or irresponsibly.

PRESSING AHEAD

Once UNAMET was on the ground, the successive decisions to press ahead, after the two short postponements of registration, were taken in full cognizance of its forthright reporting on the nature of militia violence and TNI complicity, as well as on improper government involvement in pro-autonomy activities and severe limitations on pro-independence campaigning. The reasons not to go forward were unassailable in terms of the agreements, and this might have seemed politically the safer course of action for the UN. The UN had been successfully manipulated by Indonesia in one highly dubious act of supposed self-determination in West Irian (Irian Jaya to Indonesia, West Papua to many of its inhabitants) in 1969, and it could not afford to be party to a corrupted outcome in East Timor.[2]

The Secretary-General and his Personal Representative and all the key member states were, however, determined to maintain the momentum. The political timetable in Indonesia was an important factor in their calculations. The outcome of the Indonesian elections in June made it highly uncertain that Habibie would win his own mandate when the MPR voted for a new president after August. The likely president appeared to be Megawati Sukarnoputri. Advised by former generals who were hard-liners on East Timor, she had been strongly critical of Habibie's offer of the second option and his right to make it; although she said she would respect the outcome of the consultation, she continued to urge, even as UNAMET's preparations were in full swing, that the vote be postponed until there was a government with a proper mandate in Jakarta. With Habibie himself insistent that the ballot must be held before the MPR was scheduled to be convened at the end of August, and a successor perhaps likely to embrace any excuse to abort the process, the view that there might only be a window of opportunity for self-determination in East Timor was well founded.

The desire of member states not to see the UN get bogged down in a lengthy, inconclusive, and expensive operation was a more pragmatic consideration. But the case for maintaining the momentum was more than this: East Timor was attracting unprecedented media attention and an influx of observers, both of which reinforced UNAMET as part of the scrutiny that might protect the process—and protect the East Timorese. If postponement led to their dispersal, the spotlight on East Timor might never again be as strong.

For UNAMET, the decision to go ahead was a more difficult one. Electoral staff, who had experience of other situations in which a high degree of violence and intimidation had not prevented a credible ballot, sometimes differed in their perspective from political officers. The latter's function was to analyze the extent to which Indonesia's commitments on security and a level playing field were being met, and they were in daily contact with the victims of violence. Since the conclusions of this analysis were overwhelmingly negative, they could hardly fail to question whether it was right to proceed. But they too were influenced by the immediately evident success of registration, when the East Timorese showed the strength of their own commitment to the popular consultation and the international pressure seemed to be able at least to limit the violence.

The UN consulted with key East Timorese throughout—the bishops as well as political representatives. The CNRT could always have been the ultimate arbiter; the UN could not have proceeded if the CNRT had urged that it should not. Gusmão was clear-sighted in his understanding of the risk and his mistrust of the TNI; he was also convinced that the East Timorese would defy intimidation to vote as they wanted to. He always wanted an international security force in East Timor, but he accepted the judgment that this was unattainable. The trust built up over the years between him and the Department of Political Affairs team was extended to UNAMET's decisionmaking on the ground. Marker, Vendrell, Samuel, and I made regular visits to his prison house, and whenever the UN moved forward, it did so after consulting him.

UNDERESTIMATING THE REVENGE

It is beyond doubt that the destruction of East Timor was not merely the result of an emotional response of militia and a mutiny of East Timorese within the TNI, but a planned and coordinated operation under TNI direction. The extent to which the whole chain of command was implicated in this, or to which there were dual commands operating within the TNI, may perhaps become clearer as investigations and judicial proceedings are pursued. UNAMET's failure fully to predict this, despite the warnings known to it and its expectation of substantial post-ballot violence, was shared by most diplomatic analysts but requires explanation, if not excuse.

Such an explanation is not to be found in a naïve acceptance of the Foreign Ministry's repeated assurances of a constructive transition. UNAMET was more influenced by its own experience that heavy international pressure could lead the Indonesians to rein in the violence, and by the evidence that just before the vote such pressure was being exerted and felt. In retrospect, we placed too much hope in the changes in military command and other signs that Jakarta was responsive to this pressure and in the fact that the contending East Timorese leaderships seemed to have been allowed to work together.

Our predictions rested too on a calculation of Indonesia's own self-interest. It seemed clear to objective observers that there would be a strong pro-independence vote, and at least some key Indonesian inter-locutors appeared to have understood that autonomy would lose. The fact that the ballot was allowed to proceed thus seemed to imply a reluctant acceptance of this outcome. We underestimated the extent to which many Indonesians and pro-autonomy East Timorese still believed that the coercive autonomy campaign would be successful, or nearly successful. In the context of only a narrow defeat, the removal of a large proportion of the population to West Timor, coupled with loud accusations of UNAMET bias, might have been part of a serious strate-gy to frustrate the outcome, perhaps through its rejection by the MPR. But what now appear as preparations for such a strategy—the plans for mass evacuation to West Timor—were known to UNAMET only as contingency plans, which were not improper if they were for a volun-tary exodus.

While it is certain that the postballot violence was directed by the TNI, it is not yet clear at what level it was planned and ordered. The most careful analysis of evidence available by late 2000 was made by Geoffrey Robinson, an Indonesia specialist who served as a political affairs officer in UNAMET. He concludes that the various documents that some have regarded as compelling evidence of high-level TNI planning "do not provide definitive proof of direct high-level involve-ment in planning or carrying out specific acts of violence, either before or after the ballot." The strongest evidence of TNI planning is not in documents but in the patterns of behavior of the militia, the police, and the TNI before and after the ballot, which point unequivocally to the TNI as the main center of coordination and planning. The fact that these patterns were evident in different parts of the territory suggests that coordination and planning extended at least as high as the provincial (Korem) level, and very likely higher. Senior TNI officers, including Wiranto, were well aware of the widespread and systematic violence but failed to take adequate measures to stop it. Robinson's analysis con-cludes that two related possibilities must be considered. The first is the possibility of a break or corruption of the chain of military command, entailing a loss of control by TNI headquarters over major elements of the armed forces. "A second possibility is that the violence was not the product of an explicit plan or command, but was at least in part the result of a deeply embedded pattern of thinking and behavior within the TNI."[3]

The reasons for the failure of UNAMET and others to predict events correctly can only be fully understood when and if it becomes clear how those events were set in motion.

PLANNING FOR CONTINGENCIES

The recent review of the UN's peace operations chaired by Lakhdar Brahimi (the Brahimi report) declared that "the Secretariat must not apply best-case planning assumptions to situations where the actors have historically exhibited worst-case behavior."[4] In the case of East Timor, the UN's formal planning was on the basis of a best-case scenario that the UN hoped could be realized with a high degree of international attention and pressure but that was never realistic. The UN's planning assumed—as Indonesia was promising in the negotiations— that in the event of a vote for independence, Indonesia would maintain security, administration, and budgetary support to East Timor, not just until the MPR had voted to implement the outcome but until some date perhaps months beyond that, when the UN would be ready with a transitional administration and a peacekeeping force. Although the UN regarded a vote for independence as virtually certain and thus from May onward was expecting to provide a transitional administration, almost no planning toward this was done by the UN or its agencies until the eleventh hour. The small DPA team had very limited capacity to stretch beyond its immediate responsibilities: maintaining dialogue with Indonesia and Portugal regarding the popular consultation process under way, briefing the Security Council and member states, and backstopping UNAMET. By Phase III, a full-scale peacekeeping operation would be involved, but the stage at which responsibility would pass from DPA to DPKO was not only uncertain but a matter of tension between the departments, which did not encourage a joint planning process.

DPA had proposed to DPKO in May the creation of a joint East Timor unit reporting to the heads of both departments, whose responsibilities would include coordinating planning for the later phases, but this had not received a positive response. Other UN agencies were little engaged in considering the future of East Timor. Only the World Bank engaged in serious planning and involved the CNRT and East Timorese experts in the process. The experience strongly supports the recommendation of the Brahimi report that Integrated Mission Task Forces, with members seconded from throughout the UN system as necessary, should be the standard vehicle for mission-specific planning and support.

If Phase III was barely considered, the planning for Phase II came too late to strengthen UNAMET at the time this was most needed: the immediate aftermath of the ballot. The UN's responsibility for this failure is mitigated, but not absolved, by some real external constraints: the reluctance of the Indonesians to engage in discussion of the independence option, and the U.S.-imposed delay on Security Council action. The internal constraints relating to capacity and interdepartmental planning were further handicaps. There was also a failure to plan for anything other than an official scenario that was quite unrealistically optimistic. The most positive scenario conceivable would have been limited but serious postballot violence and a faltering Indonesian effort to maintain security and administration in the face of the demoralization of their personnel. If this had occurred, the UN would have been required to move in rapidly, and its lack of preparedness for the deployment of military and civilian personnel would have been sharply exposed. In the event, if the increased numbers of CIVPOL and MLOs had joined UNAMET before 30 August, UNAMET would have been no more capable of preventing the violence and averting its own withdrawal.

The main criticism made of the UN has therefore been on a different score: the lack of contingency planning for the worst-case scenario, which became the reality. This goes to the general weakness criticized by the Brahimi report. Unless worst-case planning is insisted upon as a matter of general practice, it is hard for the Secretariat to be known to be planning for the possibility that an important member state would violate its commitment to maintain security, at a time when its friends in the Security Council were insisting on praising it for its cooperation. Even as the situation deteriorated sharply in the days after the announcement of the outcome of the ballot, the Security Council and the major powers were reluctant to signal that there should be planning for intervention. In the absence of such general practice, and without a signal from the Security Council, contingency planning for military intervention of the kind that was anathema to Indonesia could only take place outside any formal UN framework. It was because Australia had led the way in such contingency planning that the eventual intervention could be mounted so swiftly. But it may have been because Indonesia was given no reason to believe in the possibility of rapid international intervention that the TNI went so far down the path it did and so bitterly resented the crucial Australian role in making intervention possible.

THE PROTECTION DILEMMA

Nothing has done more to damage the reputation of the UN than the slaughter of civilians in the presence of its armed peacekeepers: in Rwanda and at Srebrenica. UNAMET had no armed peacekeepers and neither the means nor the mandate to protect civilians—or indeed to protect itself. Yet by encouraging the East Timorese to participate in the consultation and by promising that the UN would remain after the vote, whatever the outcome, UNAMET created expectations that the UN would afford protection, or at least would not abandon East Timor.

Amid the violence, UNAMET succeeded in evacuating its local staff, kept a team of volunteers with the IDPs who had sought shelter in its compound until they too could be flown to safety in Australia, and retained a small presence in Dili until INTERFET troops arrived. But either of two other outcomes might have occurred: UNAMET's international staff might have left East Timorese staff and IDPs behind to their fate, or the decision to remain might have resulted in international staff being killed. It was vital that the UN's commitment to the East Timorese should be fulfilled, but UNAMET had ceased to be the kind of presence that could fulfill it. The fact that all three groups in the UNAMET compound—international and local staff and the IDPs— reached safety should not be allowed to conceal the impossible dilemmas that confront a UN presence, and those responsible for its security decisions, in such circumstances. The Brahimi report rightly says that if a UN operation is given a mandate to protect civilians, it must be given the specific resources needed to carry out that mandate. But the experience of UNAMET shows that even in the absence of any such mandate, the expectations created by a UN presence may exert pressures beyond the reasonable safety of its staff. There may be no complete way out of this protection dilemma, but it points to the need for the Security Council to be willing to authorize rapid intervention to protect civilians and UN personnel and the contingency planning that can make it possible.

MOVING WITH SPEED

One of the most positive aspects of the East Timor story is the speed with which two phases of the international operations were carried out: the initial deployment of UNAMET and its rapid implementation of a complex electoral operation; and the mandating and arrival of INTER-FET. The same cannot be said of the third phase, beyond the scope of this study: the establishment of UNTAET.

The factors that permitted the first of these have been identified: the access to voluntary contributions in cash and kind that overcame normal procedures; the availability of equipment from the UN's Logistics Base; and the quality and commitment of staff able to travel immediately to the field. To these should be added excellent support arrangements in New York. The Brahimi report's recommendations aim to reform UN procedures so that these factors are not exceptional but become the norm.

Critical to the speed of intervention was the willingness of a country with a robust military capability to take the lead, aided by its proximity. But in view of Australia's requirement of a Security Council mandate and Indonesia's consent, rapid and effective diplomacy was also essential. It is impossible to attribute Indonesia's acquiescence to any single factor; what is remarkable is how well many factors worked together. They included the personal diplomacy of Secretary-General Annan and Prime Minister Howard; the fortuitous timing and use made of the APEC leaders' meeting; the strong warnings of the international financial institutions and of key member states, eventually including the United States; the Security Council mission and open meeting; and— helping to drive all of this—media coverage and the mobilization of a strong constituency of concern.

For those in East Timor, each day that passed while international intervention was under discussion was an agony, and some would argue from the recent precedent of Kosovo that a Security Council mandate need not have been awaited. Yet INTERFET was mandated only eleven days after the announcement of the result had triggered widespread violence, and it began deploying just five days after that. This represented almost unprecedented speed for international action and yet was combined with consensus decisionmaking. Whereas unauthorized intervention in Kosovo left the Security Council bitterly divided, with consequences for the eventual UN administration there, the UN's continuing role in East Timor would be founded on consensus. The Kosovo divisions themselves may have contributed to that outcome in the case of East Timor, as the Security Council strove to show that it could act in unity.

COORDINATING SUPPORT

The coordinated support of key member states, crucial to the success of a UN operation, functioned particularly well in the case of East Timor. There were periodic briefings by the Secretariat of a large and formal Secretary-General's Support Group for East Timor, with over thirty member states participating. There was no publicly announced group of Friends of the Secretary-General for East Timor, perhaps because the official nature of such groups may require some compromise between political acceptability and effectiveness. In the case of East Timor, three of the regional actors—Australia, Japan, and New Zealand—met with two permanent members of the Security Council—the United Kingdom and the United States—and the Secretariat in a self-styled Core Group.[5] The coordination ranged from the practical efforts to get UNAMET established to the critical day-by-day diplomacy in September. It was mirrored by, and linked to, the same coordination between the embassies in Jakarta. It ensured that the lead taken by the UK as drafter of Security Council statements and resolutions reflected a well-considered position of these major actors. Each of the five countries contributed personnel as well as funding to UNAMET, enhancing their engagement and their information; and their ministers, ambassadors, or senior officials visited East Timor during the consultation. From the perspective of UNAMET, the knowledge that it was an operation that commanded real commitment and understanding from member states was an important source of support in difficult circumstances.

THE VERDICT OF EAST TIMOR

As the Secretary-General's words confirm, if the international community had been able to foresee the full scale of the violence after the ballot, it could not have embarked upon the popular consultation. Yet if the judgment is right that no effort could have succeeded in 1999 in inducing Indonesia to allow a referendum in the presence of an international security force, then foreknowledge would have meant that the future of East Timor would have continued beyond 1999 to be subject to the uncertainties of the politics of Indonesia—and the future of Indonesia subject to the international politics of East Timor.

President Habibie made his decision to bring an end to the question of East Timor out of his own view of the interests of Indonesia (and in the belief that a vote for autonomy could be secured) rather than in the interests of the East Timorese. As Indonesia struggles to strengthen its new democracy amid a daunting national agenda, history may conclude that it was indeed in the interests of Indonesia that East Timor has ceased to be on that agenda. Indonesia still faces too many issues rendered almost insoluble by past actions (especially those of its armed forces); at least East Timor, with its unique implications for Indonesia's international relations, is no longer one of them.

During the twenty-four years of Indonesian occupation, East Timor suffered tens of thousands of deaths by Indonesia's admission, hundreds of thousands by the estimates of others. To these was added in 1999 the tragedy of more killings, extreme physical destruction, and the anguish of those forcibly removed to prolonged fear and squalor in West Timor. Yet, if the future of East Timor had remained unresolved within Indonesia beyond 1999, how many more might still have died before a better opportunity for self-determination could be created? Many East Timorese greeted UNAMET with the words, "We have been waiting for the United Nations for twenty-four years." It is for them to make the definitive judgment on the performance of the UN when it finally arrived, and on the further sacrifices that attended the birth of the independent nation of Timor Lorosa'e.

NOTES

1. Highlights of the briefing by Secretary-General Kofi Annan, New York, 10 September 1999.

2. The official UN account of this is in *Report of the Secretary-General Regarding the Act of Self-Determination in West Irian,* A/7723, 6 November 1969. For a recent critique, see John Saltford, "United Nations Involvement with the Act of Self-Determination in West Irian (Indonesian West New Guinea) 1968 to 1969," *Indonesia* 69 (April 2000).

3. Geoffrey Robinson, "The Fruitless Search for a Smoking Gun: Tracing the Origins of Violence in East Timor," in Freek Colombijn and Thomas Lindblad, eds., *Violence in Indonesia: Its Historical Roots and Its Contemporary Manifestations* (Leiden: KITLV Press, forthcoming).

4. *Report of the Panel on United Nations Peace Operations,* A/55/305-S/2000/809, 21 August 2000.

5. The functioning of the Core Group is described and its significance assessed by Penny Wensley, Ambassador, and Permanent Representative of Australia to the UN, in a speech, "East Timor and the United Nations," Sydney, 23 February 2000.

Appendix 1

Acronyms

ABRI	Angkatan Bersenjata Republik Indonesia (Armed Forces of the Republic of Indonesia)
AIETD	All-Inclusive Intra–East Timorese Dialogue
APEC	Asia-Pacific Economic Cooperation
Apodeti	Associação Popular Democrática Timorense (Timorese Popular Democratic Association)
ASDT	Associação Social Democrática Timor (Timorese Social Democratic Association)
BMP	Besi Merah Putih
BRTT	Barisan Rakyat Timor Timur (East Timor People's Front)
CEO	chief electoral officer
CGI	Consultative Group for Indonesia
CIVPOL	civilian police
CMLO	chief military liaison officer
CNRT	National Council of Timorese Resistance
DEO	district electoral officer
DPA	Department of Political Affairs
DPKO	Department of Peacekeeping Operations
EAD	Electoral Assistance Division
Falintil	Forças Armadas de Libertação Nacional de Timor-Leste (Armed Forces for the National Liberation of East Timor)
FPDK	Forum Persatuan, Demokrasi dan Keadilan (Forum for Unity, Democracy and Justice)
Fretilin	Frente Revolucionária de Timor Leste Independente (Revolutionary Front for an Independent East Timor)
ICRC	International Committee of the Red Cross

IDP	internally displaced person
IMF	International Monetary Fund
INTERFET	International Force for East Timor
IOM	International Organization for Migration
IPA	International Peace Academy
Komnas HAM	Indonesian National Human Rights Commission
Kopassus	Komando Pasukan Khusus (Army Special Forces Command)
Korem	Komando Resort Militer Wiradharma 164 Dili (East Timor military headquarters)
Kostrad	Komando Strategis Angkatan Darat (Army Strategic Reserve Command)
KPS	Commission on Peace and Stability
MLO	military liaison officer
MPR	Majelis Permusyawaratan Rakyat (Peoples Consultative Assembly)
NGO	nongovernmental organization
OCHA	Office for the Coordination of Humanitarian Affairs
OSCE	Organization for Security and Cooperation in Europe
PPI	Pasukan Pejuang Integrasi (Integration Struggle Troops)
PRSG	Personal Representative of the Secretary-General
SARET	Special Autonomous Region of East Timor
SRSG	Special Representative of the Secretary-General
TNI	Tentara Nasional Indonesia (Indonesian National Military)
UDT	União Democrática Timorense (Timorese Democratic Union)
UNAMET	United Nations Mission in East Timor
UNHCR	UN High Commissioner for Refugees
UNIF	Front Bersama Pro-Otonomi Timor Timur (United Front for East Timor Autonomy)
UNTAET	United Nations Transitional Administration in East Timor
UNV	United Nations Volunteer

Appendix 2

Chronology

1974	Following a change of government, Portugal acknowledges the right of the colonial territories under its administration, including East Timor, to self-determination.
1975	Civil war breaks out between those who favor independence and those who advocate integration with Indonesia. Portugal withdraws and Indonesia invades East Timor. The UN Security Council deplores the intervention and calls for Indonesian withdrawal.
1976	
17 July	Indonesia annexes East Timor as its twenty-seventh province.
1976–1981	UN General Assembly adopts annual resolutions reaffirming East Timor's right to self-determination.
1982	UN General Assembly requests the Secretary-General to hold talks with Indonesia and Portugal aimed at resolving the status of the territory. The Secretary-General reports annually on his good offices.
1991	
12 November	Santa Cruz massacre: Indonesian security forces open fire on a pro-independence demonstration of mourners at Santa Cruz cemetery, Dili.
1995	Secretary-General initiates the All-Inclusive Intra–East Timorese Dialogue.

1996	Nobel Peace Prize awarded to Bishop Belo and José Ramos-Horta.
1997	
February	Secretary-General Kofi Annan appoints Ambassador Jamsheed Marker as his personal representative for East Timor.
1998	
May	President Suharto forced to leave office.
June	President B. J. Habibie announces willingness to grant East Timor wide-ranging autonomy.
August	Tripartite negotiations on an autonomy proposal begin.
1999	
27 January	Habibie government announces "second option": East Timor to choose between autonomy or independence. Xanana Gusmão transferred from prison to prison house.
11 March	Tripartite talks reach agreement on use of a direct ballot to consult the people of East Timor.
6 April	Liquiça massacre: pro-Indonesian militia with Indonesian military kill presumed independence supporters sheltering in a church compound.
17 April	Mass gathering of pro-Indonesian militia in Dili is followed by attacks and killings at pro-independence homes.
21 April	Commission on Peace and Stability established.
5 May	Tripartite talks result in a set of agreements. Indonesia and Portugal entrust the UN with conducting a "popular consultation" to determine whether the people of East Timor accept or reject special autonomy within Indonesia.
4 June	UN flag raised at headquarters of UN mission in Dili.
11 June	Security Council formally establishes UNAMET.
18 June	Commission on Peace and Stability agrees that militias and Falintil will disarm.
22 June	Secretary-General reports that continuing violence by pro-integration militia means that the necessary conditions do not exist to begin the operational phases of the consultation process. UNAMET needs more time to deploy fully.

1999

	Opening of registration postponed by three weeks to 13 July.
25–30 June	Dare II Peace and Reconciliation Meeting in Jakarta agrees on disarmament of militia and Falintil and respect for outcome of the popular consultation, but fails to agree on procedure for follow-up.
29 June	UNAMET's Maliana office attacked by militia.
4 July	Humanitarian convoy and UN personnel attacked in Liquiça.
12 July	Delegation of Indonesian ministers visits Dili.
16 July	Voter registration begins after a three-day delay to allow Indonesian authorities to address the security situation.
25 July	239,893 East Timorese have registered in first ten days. Registration continues on the understanding that Indonesian authorities will achieve further improvements in security situation and address problem of internally displaced persons, now estimated at 60,000.
6 August	Registration closes in East Timor after two-day extension: 446,666 people registered, 433,576 in East Timor itself and 13,090 at external centers.
9 August	Campaign code of conduct signed by pro-autonomy and pro-independence organizations.
12 August	Falintil completes cantonment at four sites.
14 August	Campaigning officially launched; regional campaign committees established.
16–19 August	"Laying down of arms" at militia parades.
19–23 August	Voter lists displayed at registration centers.
22 August	East Timorese leaders from pro-autonomy and pro-independence groups agree to establish twenty-five-member commission to promote reconciliation and stability after the ballot.
26 August	Resurgence of militia violence culminates in rampage in Dili; CNRT office sacked.
27 August	Security Council extends mandate of UNAMET with increased numbers of military liaison officers and police.
29 August	Falintil and militia leaders publicly commit themselves not to carry weapons outside cantonment

1999

	sites. Indonesian police and military promise enforcement.
30 August	Polling day. Approximately 98 percent of registered voters go to the polls. UNAMET polling staff murdered at Atsabe.
31 August	East Timorese Consultative Commission meets and is boycotted by most pro-autonomy hardliners.
1 September	Militia violence and killings in Dili; journalists attacked.
2 September	Two more UNAMET local staff murdered amid militia violence in Maliana.
2–3 September	Electoral Commission considers allegations of irregularities at public hearing and concludes process not impaired.
4 September	Result of vote announced in Dili: 94,388 (21.5 percent) have voted in favor of the special autonomy proposal and 344,580 (78.5 percent) against. Campaign of violence, including killings and rape, looting and arson, launched throughout East Timor. U.S. CIVPOL officer wounded in UNAMET evacuation from Liquiça.
5 September	Wiranto and Alatas fly to Dili and are briefed by UNAMET at airport. IDPs take refuge in UNAMET's Dili compound.
6 September	Bishop Belo's house and ICRC compound attacked.
7 September	Withdrawal of UNAMET staff from regions completed.
8 September	Security Council mission begins meetings in Jakarta.
9 September	Special ministerial meeting on East Timor at APEC meeting in Auckland.
10 September	UNAMET local staff and most international staff evacuated to Darwin; eighty volunteers remain with IDPs in compound.
11 September	Security Council mission and Wiranto visit Dili. Open meeting of Security Council in New York.
12 September	Habibie announces he has called for UN assistance to restore peace and security in East Timor.

1999

14 September	IDPs from UNAMET compound evacuated to Darwin with most remaining international staff.
15 September	Security Council mandates multinational force to restore peace and security in East Timor.
20 September	First INTERFET troops land in East Timor; return of UNAMET begins.
19 October	Indonesian MPR formally decides integration of East Timor no longer applicable.
22 October	Emotional welcome for Xanana Gusmão in Dili.
25 October	Security Council mandates UNTAET.
30 October	Last Indonesian representatives leave East Timor.

Appendix 3

5 May Agreements

ANNEX 1: AGREEMENT BETWEEN THE REPUBLIC OF INDONESIA AND THE PORTUGUESE REPUBLIC ON THE QUESTION OF EAST TIMOR

The Governments of Indonesia and Portugal,

Recalling General Assembly resolutions 1514(XV), 1541(XV), 2625(XXV) and the relevant resolutions and decisions adopted by the Security Council and the General Assembly on the questions of East Timor;

Bearing in mind the sustained efforts of the Governments of Indonesia and Portugal since July 1983, through the good offices of the Secretary-General, to find a just, comprehensive and internationally acceptable solution to the question of East Timor;

Recalling the agreement of 5 August 1998 to undertake, under the auspices of the Secretary-General, negotiations on a special status based on a wide-ranging autonomy for East Timor without prejudice to the positions of principle of the respective Governments on the final status of East Timor;

Having discussed a constitutional framework for an autonomy for East Timor on the basis of a draft presented by the United Nations, as amended by the Indonesian Government;

Noting the position of the Government of Indonesia that the proposed special autonomy should be implemented only as an end solution to the

141

question of East Timor with full recognition of Indonesian sovereignty over East Timor;

Noting the position of the Government of Portugal that an autonomy regime should be transitional, not requiring recognition of Indonesian sovereignty over East Timor or the removal of East Timor from the list of Non-Self-Governing Territories of the General Assembly, pending a final decision on the status of East Timor by the East Timorese people through an act of self-determination under United Nations auspices;

Taking into account that, although the Governments of Indonesia and Portugal each have their positions of principle on the prepared proposal for special autonomy, both agree that it is essential to move the peace process forward, and that therefore, the Governments of Indonesia and Portugal agree that the Secretary-General should consult the East Timorese people on the constitutional framework for autonomy attached hereto as an annex;

Bearing in mind that the Governments of Indonesia and Portugal requested the Secretary-General to devise the method and procedures for the popular consultation through direct, secret and universal ballot;

Agree as follows,

Article 1. Request the Secretary-General to put the attached proposed constitutional framework providing for a special autonomy for East Timor within the unitary Republic of Indonesia to the East Timorese people, both inside and outside East Timor, for their consideration and acceptance or rejection through a popular consultation on the basis of a direct, secret and universal ballot.

Article 2. Request the Secretary-General to establish, immediately after the signing of this Agreement, an appropriate United Nations mission in East Timor to enable him to effectively carry out the popular consultation.

Article 3. The Government of Indonesia will be responsible for maintaining peace and security in East Timor in order to ensure that the popular consultation is carried out in a fair and peaceful way in an atmosphere free of intimidation, violence or interference from any side.

Article 4. Request the Secretary-General to report the result of the popular consultation to the Security Council and the General Assembly, as well as to inform the Governments of Indonesia and Portugal and the East Timorese people.

Article 5. If the Secretary-General determines, on the basis of the result of the popular consultation and in accordance with this Agreement, that, the proposed constitutional framework for special autonomy is acceptable to the East Timorese people, the Government of Indonesia shall initiate the constitutional measures necessary for the implementation of the constitutional framework, and the Government of Portugal shall initiate within the United Nations the procedures necessary for the removal of East Timor from the list of Non-Self-Governing Territories of the General Assembly and the deletion of the question of East Timor from the agendas of the Security Council and the General Assembly.

Article 6. If the Secretary-General determines, on the basis of the result of the popular consultation and in accordance with this Agreement, that the proposed constitutional framework for special autonomy is not acceptable to the East Timorese people, the Government of Indonesia shall take the constitutional steps necessary to terminate its links with East Timor thus restoring under Indonesian law the status East Timor held prior to 17 July 1976, and the Governments of Indonesia and Portugal and the Secretary-General shall agree on arrangements for a peaceful and orderly transfer of authority in East Timor to the United Nations. The Secretary-General shall, subject to the appropriate legislative mandate, initiate the procedure enabling East Timor to begin a process of transition towards independence.

Article 7. During the interim period between the conclusion of the popular consultation and the start of the implementation of either option, the parties request the Secretary-General to maintain an adequate United Nations presence in East Timor.

Done in New York, on this 5th day of May 1999.

Ali Alatas
Minister of Foreign Affairs, Government of Indonesia

Jaime Gama
Minister of Foreign Affairs, Government of Portugal

Kofi A. Annan
Secretary-General, United Nations

ANNEX II: AGREEMENT REGARDING THE MODALITIES FOR THE POPULAR CONSULTATION OF THE EAST TIMORESE THROUGH A DIRECT BALLOT

The Governments of Indonesia and Portugal and the Secretary-General of the United Nations, agree as follows:

Immediately following the conclusion of the agreement between the two Governments requesting the Secretary-General to consult the East Timorese people on whether they would accept or reject the proposed constitutional framework for autonomy, the Secretary-General will, subject to the appropriate legislative mandate, begin preparations for the popular consultation by deploying in East Timor such personnel as will be adequate for the purpose of executing the various phases of the consultation process. Preparations for the vote outside East Timor will also begin at locations of major East Timorese concentration outside of East Timor.

A. Date for consultation. The ballot will take place on Sunday, 8 August 1999, both inside and outside East Timor.

B. Question to be put before the voters. The question that the Secretary-General will put to the voters is:

> Do you *accept* the proposed special autonomy for East Timor within the Unitary State of the Republic of Indonesia?   ACCEPT ❑
> OR
> Do you *reject* the proposed special autonomy for East Timor, leading to East Timor's separation from Indonesia?   REJECT ❑

The United Nations logo will appear on the ballot papers. The ballot papers will include symbols to facilitate voting by illiterate persons.

C. Entitlement to vote. The following persons, aged 17 years or above, shall be eligible to vote in the popular consultation: (a) persons born in East Timor, (b) persons born outside East Timor but with at least one parent having been born in East Timor, and (c) persons whose spouses fall under either of the two categories above.

D. Schedule of the consultation process (in overlapping time periods). The schedule for the operational stages of the consultation process will be approximately as follows:

Operational planning/Deployment	10 May–15 June
Public information programme/ Voter education	10 May–5 August
Preparation and Registration	13 June–17 July
Exhibition of lists and challenges/ Decisions on challenges and complaints	18 July–23 July
Political Campaign	20 July–5 August*
Cooling off period	6 August–7 August
Polling Day	8 August

* Subject to revision

E. Operational Phases.

a. Information Campaign.

- The United Nations will make available the text of the main Agreement and the autonomy document to be voted on in the following languages: Tetun, Bahasa Indonesia, Portuguese and English.
- The United Nations will disseminate and explain the content of the main Agreement and the autonomy document in an impartial and factual manner inside and outside East Timor.
- The United Nations will explain to voters the process and procedure of the vote, and the implications of an "accept" or "reject" vote.
- The radio stations and the newspapers in East Timor as well as other Indonesian and Portuguese media outlets will be utilized in the dissemination of this information. Other appropriate means of dissemination will be made use of as required.

b. Registration.

- Registration inside and outside East Timor will take place for a continuous period of 20 days.
- Two hundred registration centres will be opened in East Timor for this purpose.
- Outside East Timor, special registration centres will be opened in Jakarta, Yogyakarta, Surabaya, Denpasar, Ujung Pandang, Sydney, Darwin, Perth, Melbourne, Lisbon, Maputo, Macau, New York with adjustments to be made as appropriate. The United Nations may utilize the services of the Australian Electoral

Commission for balloting in Australia and of the International Organization for Migration (IOM) in Portugal and elsewhere.

- The registration lists will be exhibited for five days at the end of the registration period at the respective registration centres, regional offices and at Dili headquarters. Challenges to the lists shall be submitted to the regional offices for a final decision by the Electoral Commission prior to polling day.

c. Campaign.

- Supporters and opponents of the autonomy proposal will campaign ahead of the vote in a peaceful and democratic manner during the period designated for this purpose.
- There will be a Code of Conduct for the campaign, to be proposed by the United Nations and discussed with the supporters and opponents of the autonomy proposal.
- The United Nations will devise the means to provide equal opportunity for the two sides to disseminate their views to the public.
- Officials of the Governments of Indonesia and Portugal will not participate in the campaign in support of either option.
- East Timorese government officials may campaign in their personal capacity. All such campaigning will be carried out strictly according to the Code of Conduct without use of public funds and government resources or recourse to pressure of office.

d. Balloting in East Timor.

- Voting in East Timor will take place in approximately 700 registration/polling stations located in 200 polling centres.

e. Balloting outside East Timor.

- Voting will take place in polling stations set up in the same locations as the registration centres mentioned above.

f. Observers.

- Indonesia and Portugal shall be entitled to send an equal number of representatives to observe all the operational phases of the consultation process both inside and outside East Timor.
- International observers will be able to observe the consultation process under terms to be developed by the United Nations to regulate their presence.

F. Funding. The Secretary-General will seek the approval of the Security Council for the operation in order to ensure assessed budgetary funding. Voluntary contributions will be channeled through a Trust Fund established for this purpose.

G. Security. The Indonesian authorities will ensure a secure environment for a free and fair popular consultation process and will be responsible for the security of United Nations personnel. A number of United Nations security guards will be deployed to ensure the security and safety of the United Nations personnel and property. A number of international civilian police will be available in East Timor to advise the Indonesian Police during the operational phases of the popular consultation and, at the time of the consultation, to supervise the escort of ballot papers and boxes to and from polling sites.

Done in New York on this 5th day of May 1999.

Ali Alatas
Minister of Foreign Affairs, Government of Indonesia

Jaime Gama
Minister of Foreign Affairs, Government of Portugal

Kofi A. Annan
Secretary-General, United Nations

* * *

ANNEX III: EAST TIMOR POPULAR CONSULTATION

The Governments of Indonesia and Portugal and the Secretary-General of the United Nations, agree as follows:

1. A secure environment devoid of violence or other forms of intimidation is a prerequisite for the holding of a free and fair ballot in East Timor. Responsibility to ensure such an environment as well as for the general maintenance of law and order rests with the appropriate Indonesian security authorities. The absolute neutrality of the TNI (Indonesian Armed Forces) and the Indonesian Police is essential in this regard.

2. The Commission on Peace and Stability established in Dili on 21 April 1999 should become operational without delay. The Commission, in cooperation with the United Nations, will elaborate a code of conduct, by which all parties should abide, for the period prior to and following the consultation, ensure the laying down of arms and take the necessary steps to achieve disarmament.

3. Prior to the start of the registration, the Secretary-General shall ascertain, based on the objective evaluation of the UN mission, that the necessary security situation exists for the peaceful implementation of the consultation process.

4. The police will be solely responsible for the maintenance of law and order. The Secretary-General, after obtaining the necessary mandate, will make available a number of civilian police officers to act as advisers to the Indonesian Police in the discharge of their duties and, at the time of the consultation, to supervise the escort of ballot papers and boxes to and from polling sites.

Done in New York on this 5th day of May 1999.

Ali Alatas
Minister of Foreign Affairs, Government of Indonesia

Jaime Gama
Minister of Foreign Affairs, Government of Portugal

Kofi A. Annan
Secretary-General, United Nations

Appendix 4

UN Security Council
Resolution 1246, 11 June 1999

RESOLUTION 1246 (1999): ADOPTED BY THE
SECURITY COUNCIL AT ITS 4013TH MEETING
ON 11 JUNE 1999

The Security-Council,

Recalling its previous resolutions on the situation in East Timor, in particular resolution 1236 (1999) of 7 May 1999,

Recalling the Agreement between Indonesia and Portugal on the question of East Timor of 5 May 1999 (the General Agreement) and the Agreements between the United Nations and the Governments of Indonesia and Portugal of the same date regarding the modalities for the popular consultation on the East Timorese through a direct ballot and regarding security arrangements (the Security Agreement) (S/1999/513, annexes I–III),

Welcoming the report of the Secretary-General on the Question of East Timor of 22 May 1999 (S/1999/595),

Noting with concern the assessment of the Secretary-General contained in that report that the security situation in East Timor remains "extremely tense and volatile,"

Taking note of the pressing need for reconciliation between the various competing factions within East Timor,

Welcoming the fruitful cooperation of the Government of Indonesia and the local authorities in East Timor with the United Nations,

Taking note of the letter from the Permanent Representative of Portugal to the United Nations to the President of the Security Council of 7 June 1999 (S/1999/652),

Welcoming the conclusion of consultations between the Government of Indonesia and the United Nations on the deployment of military liaison officers within the mission established by this resolution,

Bearing in mind the sustained efforts of the Governments of Indonesia and Portugal since July 1983, through the good offices of the Secretary-General, to find a just, comprehensive and internationally acceptable solution to the question of East Timor,

Welcoming the appointment of the Special Representative of the Secretary-General for the East Timor Popular Consultation, and reiterating its support for the efforts of the Personal Representative of the Secretary-General for East Timor,

1. *Decides* to establish until 31 August 1999 the United Nations Mission in East Timor (UNAMET) to organize and conduct a popular consultation, scheduled for 8 August 1999, on the basis of a direct, secret and universal ballot, in order to ascertain whether the East Timorese people accept the proposed constitutional framework providing for a special autonomy for East Timor within the unitary Republic of Indonesia or reject the proposed special autonomy for East Timor, leading to East Timor's separation from Indonesia, in accordance with the General Agreement and to enable the Secretary-General to discharge his responsibility under paragraph 3 of the Security Agreement;

2. *Authorizes* until 31 August 1999 the deployment within UNAMET of up to 280 civilian police officers to act as advisers to the Indonesian Police in the discharge of their duties and, at the time of the consultation, to supervise the escort of ballot papers and boxes to and from the polling sites;

3. *Authorizes* until 31 August 1999 the deployment within UNAMET of 50 military liaison officers to maintain contact with the Indonesian Armed Forces in order to allow the Secretary-General to discharge his responsibilities under the General Agreement and the Security Agreement;

4. *Endorses* the Secretary-General's proposal that UNAMET should also incorporate the following components:

a. a political component responsible for monitoring the fairness of the political environment, for ensuring the freedom of all political and other non-governmental organizations to carry out their activities freely and for monitoring and advising the Special Representative on all matters with political implications,

b. an electoral component responsible for all activities related to registration and voting,

c. an information component responsible for explaining to the East Timorese people, in an objective and impartial manner without prejudice to any position or outcome, the terms of the General Agreement and the proposed autonomy framework, for providing information on the process and procedure of the vote and for explaining the implications of a vote in favour or against the proposal;

5. *Notes* the intention of the Governments of Indonesia and Portugal to send an equal number of representatives to observe all the operational phases of the consultation process both inside and outside East Timor;

6. *Welcomes* the intention of the Secretary-General to conclude with the Government of Indonesia, as soon as possible, a status-of-mission agreement and *urges* the early conclusion of negotiations with a view to the full and timely deployment of UNAMET;

7. *Calls upon* all parties to cooperate with UNAMET in the implementation of its mandate, and to ensure the security and freedom of movement of its staff in carrying out that mandate in all areas of East Timor;

8. *Approves* the modalities for the implementation of the popular consultation process scheduled for 8 August 1999 as set out in paragraphs 15 to 18 of the report of the Secretary-General of 22 May 1999;

9. *Stresses once again* the responsibility of the Government of Indonesia to maintain peace and security in East Timor, in particular in the present security situation referred to in the report of the Secretary-General, in order to ensure that the popular consultation is carried out in a fair and peaceful way and in an atmosphere free of intimidation, violence or interference from any side and to ensure the safety and security of United Nations and other international staff and observers in East Timor;

10. *Welcomes in this regard* the decision taken by the Government of Indonesia to establish a ministerial team to monitor and ensure the security of the popular consultation in accordance with Article 3 of the General Agreement and paragraph 1 of the Security Agreement;

11. *Condemns* all acts of violence from whatever quarter and *calls*

for an end to such acts and the laying down of arms by all armed groups in East Timor, for the necessary steps to achieve disarmament and for further steps in order to ensure a secure environment devoid of violence or other forms of intimidation, which is a prerequisite for the holding of a free and fair ballot in East Timor;

12. *Requests* all parties to ensure that conditions exist for the comprehensive implementation of the popular consultation, with the full participation of the East Timorese people;

13. *Urges* that every effort be made to make the Commission on Peace and Stability operative, and in particular *stresses* the need for the Indonesian authorities to provide security and personal protection for members of the Commission in cooperation with UNAMET;

14. *Reiterates* its request to the Secretary-General to keep the Security Council closely informed of the situation, and to continue to report to it every fourteen days on the implementation of its resolutions and of the Tripartite Agreements and on the security situation in East Timor;

15. *Decides* to remain seized of the matter.

Appendix 5

UN Security Council Resolution 1264, 15 September 1999

RESOLUTION 1264 (1999): ADOPTED BY THE
SECURITY COUNCIL AT ITS 4045TH MEETING
ON 15 SEPTEMBER 1999

The Security-Council,

Recalling its previous resolutions and the statements of its President on the situation in East Timor,

Recalling also the Agreement between Indonesia and Portugal on the question of East Timor of 5 May 1999 and the Agreements between the United Nations and the Governments of Indonesia and Portugal of the same date regarding the modalities for the popular consultation of the East Timorese through a direct ballot and security arrangements (S/1999/513, Annexes I to III),

Reiterating its welcome for the successful conduct of the popular consultation of the East Timorese people of 30 August 1999 and *taking note* of its outcome, which it regards as an accurate reflection of the views of the East Timorese people,

Deeply concerned by the deterioration in the security situation in East Timor, and in particular by the continuing violence against and large-scale displacement and relocation of East Timorese civilians,

Deeply concerned also at the attacks on the staff and premises of the

United Nations Mission in East Timor (UNAMET), on other officials and on the international and national humanitarian personnel,

Recalling the relevant principles contained in the Convention on the Safety of United Nations and Associated Personnel adopted on 9 December 1994,

Appalled by the worsening humanitarian situation in East Timor, particularly as it affects women, children and other vulnerable groups,

Reaffirming the right of refugees and displaced persons to return in safety and security to their homes,

Endorsing the report of the Security Council Mission to Jakarta and Dili (S/1999/976),

Welcoming the statement by the President of Indonesia on 12 September 1999 in which he expressed readiness of Indonesia to accept an international peacekeeping force through the United Nations in East Timor,

Welcoming the letter from the Minister for Foreign Affairs of Australia to the Secretary-General of 14 September 1999 (S/1999/975),

Reaffirming respect for the sovereignty and territorial integrity of Indonesia,

Expressing its concern at reports indicating that systematic, widespread and flagrant violations of international humanitarian and human rights law have been committed in East Timor, and *stressing* that persons committing such violations bear individual responsibility,

Determining that the present situation in East Timor constitutes a threat to peace and security,

Acting under Chapter VII of the Charter of the United Nations,

 1. *Condemns* all acts of violence in East Timor, *calls* for their immediate end and *demands* that those responsible for such acts be brought to justice;
 2. *Emphasizes* the urgent need for coordinated humanitarian assistance and the importance of allowing full, safe and unimpeded access by humanitarian organizations and *calls upon* all parties to cooperate

with such organizations so as to ensure the protection of civilians at risk, the safe return of refugees and displaced persons and the effective delivery of humanitarian aid;

3. *Authorizes* the establishment of a multinational force under a unified command structure, pursuant to the request of the Government of Indonesia conveyed to the Secretary-General on 12 September 1999, with the following tasks: to restore peace and security in East Timor, to protect and support UNAMET in carrying out its tasks and, within force capabilities, to facilitate humanitarian assistance operations, and *authorizes* the States participating in the multinational force to take all necessary measures to fulfil this mandate;

4. *Welcomes* the expressed commitment of the Government of Indonesia to cooperate with the multinational force in all aspects of the implementation of its mandate and *looks forward* to close coordination between the multinational force and the Government of Indonesia;

5. *Underlines* the Government of Indonesia's continuing responsibility under the Agreements of 5 May 1999, taking into account the mandate of the multinational force set out in paragraph 3 above, to maintain peace and security in East Timor in the interim phase between the conclusion of the popular consultation and the start of the implementation of its result and to guarantee the security of the personnel and premises of UNAMET;

6. *Welcomes* the offers by Member States to organize, lead and contribute to the multinational force in East Timor, *calls on* Member States to make further contributions of personnel, equipment and other resources and *invites* Member States in a position to contribute to inform the leadership of the multinational force and the Secretary-General;

7. *Stresses* that it is the responsibility of the Indonesian authorities to take immediate and effective measures to ensure the safe return of refugees to East Timor;

8. *Notes* that Article 6 of the Agreement of 5 May 1999 states that the Governments of Indonesia and Portugal and the Secretary-General shall agree on arrangements for a peaceful and orderly transfer of authority in East Timor to the United Nations, and *requests* the leadership of the multinational force to cooperate closely with the United Nations to assist and support those arrangements;

9. *Stresses* that the expenses for the force will be borne by the participating Member States concerned and *requests* the Secretary-General to establish a trust fund through which contributions could be channeled to the States or operations concerned;

10. *Agrees* that the multinational force should collectively be

deployed in East Timor until replaced as soon as possible by a United Nations peacekeeping operation, and *invites* the Secretary-General to make prompt recommendations on a peacekeeping operation to the Security Council;

11. *Invites* the Secretary-General to plan and prepare for a United Nations transitional administration in East Timor, incorporating a United Nations peacekeeping operation, to be deployed in the implementation phase of the popular consultation (phase III) and to make recommendations as soon as possible to the Security Council;

12. *Requests* the leadership of the multinational force to provide periodic reports on progress towards the implementation of its mandate through the Secretary-General to the Council, the first such report to be made within 14 days of the adoption of this resolution;

13. *Decides* to remain actively seized of the matter.

Appendix 6

Electoral Commission Determination

The directions for voting, the registration process and the polling were conducted in accordance with the New York Agreements. The popular consultation provides an accurate reflection of the will of the people of East Timor.

Their rejection of the proposed framework is clear:

Votes in favour of acceptance of the proposed constitutional framework	94,388
Percentage	21.5
Votes in favour of rejection of the proposed constitutional framework	344,580
Percentage	78.5
Number of invalid notes	7,985
Percentage	1.8
Total number of ballot papers counted	446,953

Pat Bradley
Johann Kriegler
Bong-Scuk Sohn
Dili, 4 September 1999

* * *

REASONS FOR DETERMINATION

1. The Electoral Commission was appointed by the Secretary-General pursuant to the New York Agreements. Its mandates principally entailed two tasks:

- to ensure that the directions for voting, the registration process and the polling are conducted in accordance with the Modalities Agreement; and
- to determine whether in its opinion the consultation has been able to provide an accurate reflection of the will of the people of East Timor.

2. The three commissioners were able to oversee the whole of the consultative process from the commencement of the registration to the conclusion of the count. They enjoyed unstinting support from the Special Representative of the Secretary-General and the whole of the UNAMET contingent. They also established and maintained cordial relations with all significant role players in the consultation, more especially the two Official Observer Missions, the main political protagonists and the vast number of intergovernmental, international and local electoral observer groups. Liaison was also initiated with humanitarian agencies, the Catholic Church and several nongovernmental organizations.

3. From the outset the commissioners were able to evaluate the evolving regulatory framework, and the implementation of the administrative design, developed by the Chief Electoral Officer and his personnel. The Commission is satisfied that both were theoretically sound and properly implemented. In particular the Commission wishes to endorse the decision to rely heavily on local staff for the manning of the voting centres. It also wishes to commend the Chief Electoral Officer for the flexibility displayed in dealing with the fluid situation that developed when tens of thousands of voters fled from their homes in the face of violence. Ultimately the voter turn-out figure of over 98 percent evidences the competence of the administration.

4. The commissioners made it their business, between them, to visit as many of the registration/voting centres as was possible during July and August. They also continuously monitored the process by consultations with observer groups and UNAMET staff and also by analysing the increasing volume of written reports emanating from all quarters. More particularly the Commission considered a steady stream of objections and complaints about irregularities, real or perceived. During the

count the Commission afforded the pro-autonomy umbrella organization, UNIF, a hearing of a day and a half to present argument and evidence in support of its contention that polling had been marred by a number of administrative irregularities. The Chief Electoral Officer was given an opportunity to meet such charges. The Commission concluded that, whatever merit there might be in individual complaints regarding alleged misconduct and/or partiality on the part of the electoral staff none of them, singly or collectively, impaired the process as such. No election is perfect and, having regard to the circumstances, the instant electoral process was a singular achievement. It is a pity that active and creative participation of the two opposed political groupings could never be properly marshaled. In the result the political parties, especially the losers, lacked a sense of co-ownership of the process. This lies at the root of their complaints and served as a trigger for violence. Even with the wisdom of hindsight it must be acknowledged that this was unavoidable in the context of preventing strife and bloodshed.

5. Nevertheless, it is less than four months since the historic New York Agreements opened a new avenue of hope for the people of East Timor. In that remarkably short space of time UNAMET was established, took up its task and has today concluded the first crucial phase of the journey. That was for the Secretary-General to put to those people, for their consideration and acceptance or rejection, a proposed constitutional framework for their special autonomy within the unitary Republic of Indonesia. He was to devise the method and procedures for a popular consultation on the basis of a direct, secret and universal ballot.

6. The consultation, consisting of four interrelated steps, has run its course. First there was the compilation of a voters' roll, which was successfully performed during July and August 1999. Voters' rolls were created listing 451,792 voters in 885 voting districts within the territory and in Australia, Indonesia, Macau, Maputo, New York and Portugal. The database thus generated was not only a sound basis for the consultation but will prove of great value in future elections as well as in the general administration of East Timor.

7. Next there was to have been a public debate between the supporters of the constitutional framework and its opponents, so that the electorate could make a considered choice. To this end the Indonesian Government was to have ensured a secure environment, free of intimidation, violence or interference, while its civilian and security agencies were enjoined to maintain strict neutrality. Regrettably, that was not to be. Murder, arson, terror and mob violence, largely if not wholly committed by the pro-autonomy militias, went unchecked. Prominent pro-

autonomy leaders threatened a bloodbath should they lose, while pro-independence offices were sacked and a prominent leader assassinated.

8. The third step was the actual polling, which took place on Monday, 30 August 1999. Although polling had to be suspended in seven centres because of violence by pro-autonomy supporters, each and every centre concluded its work on polling day. In all, 438,968 voters cast their votes in East Timor and abroad. The turn-out was an astonishing 98.6 percent. Even more striking was the manifest determination of the people to vote. Many centres reported hundreds of voters waiting at dawn; at some there were thousands. Consequently balloting was often completed by the early afternoon. Notwithstanding the urgency with which the poll had to be organised, and disruption of recruiting and training of local staff due to violence, polling was generally orderly and efficient after a frantic start.

9. Then followed step four: the count, which was conducted at a central counting station in Dili. Upon conclusion of the poll all voting centres substantially complied with the prescribed procedure for the accounting, recording, sealing and dispatch of voting materials by helicopter to the counting station. At one centre pro-autonomy elements temporarily impeded the dispatch of material but all ballot boxes were duly accounted for at the counting station by Wednesday, 1 September 1999. The prescribed procedures for the verification of voting materials ensued, followed by the sorting of ballot papers and the count. The decision to conduct centralised counting was volubly condemned by the Indonesian Official Observer Mission as well as by UNIF. The Commission has no hesitation in supporting the decision. The level of intimidation and threat of violence was such that decentralised counting would have been folly. Indeed, supervening events show it would have been disastrous.

10. It is for these reasons that the Commission was able to declare that the popular consultation had been procedurally fair and in accordance with the New York Agreements, and consequently provided an accurate reflection of the will of the people of East Timor. There can be no doubt that the overwhelming majority of the people of this troubled land wish to separate from the Republic of Indonesia.

Pat Bradley
Johann Kriegler
Bong-Scuk Sohn
Dili, 4 September 1999

Index

Affidavits, 54, 57
Agam, Hasmy, 105
Aitarak, 24–25, 46
Alatas, Ali, 31, 91; APEC meeting, 107; central count, 88; commitment to postballot peace, 83, 122; Dare II meeting, 68; 5 May Agreements, signing of, 33; international force, 97, 105, 112–114; militia attacks, 26, 51*n11*, 93; peace commission, 29–30; special autonomy proposal, 22, 24, 26; visit to Dili (12 July 1999), 48; visit to Dili (5 Sept. 1999), 96, 104; voter intimidation allegations, 92; voting methods, 28
Albright, Madeleine, 85, 107–108
All-Inclusive Intra–East Timorese Dialogue (AIETD), 18–19, 67
Amnesty International, 13
Andjaba, Martin, 105, 110
Andrews, David, 26
Annan, Kofi: Australian command of INTERFET, 113; ballot postponement, 46; crimes against humanity, 111; Electoral Commission, 61; 5 May Agreements, 33–34, 121; Gusmão release, 74; human rights, 115, 121; IDP evacuation, 101; international force, 104–105, 109, 112; Popular Consultation, 11; reports and letters to Security Council, 37, 46, 49, 50, 56, 57, 80–81; security arrangements, 12, 32, 37, 49; UN role in East Timor, 18; UNAMET, 37, 80, 85, 99; voter registration, 57;

UNAMET evacuation, 99–101; voting results announcement, 11, 93–94
Antara, 48
Apodeti, 15–16
Armed Forces for the National Liberation of East Timor (Falintil), 20, 29, 31, 44, 48, 71; as armed wing of Fretilin, 17; cantonment of, 72–73; Commission on Peace and Stability, 70; disarmament, 68, 77; response to TNI-militia violence, 30, 97; security arrangements, 32; under arms, 47; voter registration for members of, 59
Army Strategic Reserve Command (Kostrad), 94, 98, 100–101, 110
Asia-Pacific Economic Cooperation (APEC) meeting, 106–107, 113
Association of Southeast Asian Nations, 112
Australia, 83; contingency planning by, 127; closure of consulate, 98; Core Group, 130; electoral observers, 88; Indonesian stability as interest of, 120; integration commitment, 20–21; INTERFET, 103, 108–109, 112–113; international force, 106, 109; security arrangements, 33, 48; standby military forces, 103
Australian Defense Force, 98
Australian Electoral Commission, 38, 54, 59
Australian Labor Party, 20
Axworthy, Lloyd, 107

Bahrain, 120

Belo, Bishop Carlos Filipe Ximenes: attack on house of, 96, 106; campaign code of conduct, 62; Dare I and Dare II, 67–68; evacuation of, 96; Nobel Peace prize award, 17; peace commission, 29; referendum on independence, 23

Beng Yong Chew, 40

Berger, Sandy, 109

Besi Merah Putih (BMP), 24, 25, 100

Blood-drinking ceremonies, 44

Bradley, Pat, 61

Brahimi report (Lakhdar Brahimi), 126–129

Brazil, 88

Brimob, 71

Cambodia, 42, 109

Camdessus, Michel, 108

Campaign rallies, 73, 75–76

Canada, 88, 107, 112–113

Carnation Revolution, 15

Carrascalão, Manuel, 25–26, 70

Carter Center, 56

Carvalho, Cancio de, 73

Catholic Church, 96, 106

Cesario Belo, Joanico, 70, 77

Chief Electoral Officer (CEO), 48, 54, 60, 61, 63, 92

Chile, 88

CIVPOL. *See* United Nations Civilian Police (CIVPOL)

Clinton, Bill, 85, 108–109

CNRT. *See* National Council of Timorese Resistance (CNRT)

Cohen, William, 85, 109

Commission on Peace and Stability (KPS), 30–31; cantonment monitoring, 78; local visits, 71; nonviolence agreement, 70; reconciliation, 97; weaknesses of, 70

Conflict management bodies, 29

Congress, U.S.: authorization of UN missions, 39, 81, 113; visit of delegation to Suai, 77

Consultative Group for Indonesia (CGI), 107–108

Cook, Robin, 107

Core Group, 85, 109, 130

Cosgrove, Maj. Gen. Peter, 114

Costa, José da, 97

Crimes against humanity, 100, 111

Damiri, Maj.-Gen. Adam, 30, 57, 73, 100

Dare I Peace and Reconciliation Meeting, 67–68

Dare II Peace and Reconciliation Meeting, 63, 68

Department of Peacekeeping Operations (DPKO), 38, 72, 126; Field Administration and Logistics Division, 40

Department of Political Affairs (DPA), 38, 126; Asia and Pacific Division, 28, 40; Electoral Assistance Division (EAD), 28–29, 40, 53–54

Disarmament, 33, 68, 70–72, 77

District Electoral Officers (DEOs), 53; attacks on, 47, 77; on ballot day, 89; in the postballot period, 80; preparation for voting, 87; recruitment, 42; training, 41; voter information campaign role, 55, 87

Downer, Alexander, 104, 107–108

Dutch East Indies, 16

East Timor, 16: electoral observers from, 88; independence, 130–131; Kosovo conflict compared to, 119–120; partitioning of, 88; political divisions, 50n7; as Portuguese overseas province, 15; role in negotiations, 21; transitional arrangements, 19

East Timor People's Front (BRTT), 43–44, 62

East Timor Student Solidarity Council, 75

East Timorese Consultative Commission, 69–70, 74, 93

East Timorese Regional Council, 27

Elections: Cambodia (1993), 53–54; Indonesia (1999), 29, 53–54, 123. *See also* Popular Consultation

Electoral Commission: appointment of, 38, 60–61; central count, 88; electoral observers, 89; paramilitary violence, 83; voter intimidation hearings, 91–92; voter registration, 11, 61

Electoral Directions, 54

European Union (EU): arms boycott of

Indonesia, 109; election observers, 88; Indonesian stability as interest of, 120; international force, 107; Kosovo, 119; special autonomy proposal, 22; UNAMET funding by, 39

Falintil. *See* Armed Forces for the National Liberation of East Timor (Falintil)
Fischer, Jeff (CEO), 40, 88–89, 91
5 May Agreements: campaign code of conduct, 62–63; Indonesian elections as factor in, 29; Indonesian security responsibilities, 12; presentation to the security council of, 37; signing of, 11, 33–34; UNAMET report of violations of, 44; weaknesses, 121–122
Forum for Unity, Democracy and Justice (FPDK), 43–44, 47, 62, 70, 93
Fretilin. *See* Revolutionary Front for an Independent East Timor (Fretilin)

G–77, 120
Gama, Jaime, 33, 106
Garnadi, Maj. Gen. H. R., 82
Greenstock, Jeremy, 105
Gulf War, 109
Gusmão, José Alexandre "Xanana," 20; campaign code of conduct, 63; capture of, 17; Commission on Peace and Stability, 29, 31, 70; Dare II meeting, 68; disarmament, 70, 71–72, 77; draft proposals for autonomy, 26; East Timor leaders meetings, 69–70; Falintil response to militias, 30, 97; independence referendum, 23; international force, 104; joint campaign proposal, 63–64; move to house arrest, 21–22, 74; nonviolence agreement, 70; peace commission, 29–31; release of, 19, 69, 73–74, 106; return to East Timor, 115; security arrangements, 32; suspension of voting process, possible, 50; TNI troop reduction, 71; transitional arrangements, 19; UN consultation with, 38, 124; voter registration by, 58; voter registration extension, 60; voting methods, 28

Guterres, Antonio, 106
Guterres, Eurico: East Timor leaders meeting, 70; as head of Pam Swakarsa, 46; occupation of Dili airport by, 93; regional commanders meeting, 77; TNI arming of militias, 25

Habibie, B. J., 32, 48; APEC meeting, 107; commitment to postballot peace, 83; elections in Indonesia, 29, 123; Gusmão release, 74; humanitarian aid, 58; Indonesian security responsibilities, 12; international force, 97, 104–106, 109, 111–112; letters from Howard, 21–22; militia attacks, 26; peacekeeping operation, 33; Popular Consultation, 30, 121–122, 130; security arrangements, 31; special autonomy proposal, 19; UNAMET evacuation, 99–100; U.S. report on paramilitary violence, 77; voter registration postponement, 45; withdrawal of Zacky by, 77, 84
Haiti, 113
Halilintar, 24–25
Hamer, Alphons, 105
Hawk fighters, 109
Howard, John, 129; IDP evacuation, 101; international force, 104, 108, 113; letter to Habibie, 21–22, 24; peacekeeping operation, 33; policy review, 20; Popular Consultation, 30; security arrangements, 32
Human rights: Indonesian violations, 17–18; inquiry into violations, 115; as motive for intervention, 121; paramilitary violations, 25; Samuel report, 29; UN joint mission, 102$n6$; UNAMET role, 38; UNTAET investigations, 102$n6$
Humanitarian aid, 58, 115

Independence: Indonesian view, 125; Indonesian warnings about, 81–82; proclamations of, 16; referendum on, 23; UN position, 126
Indonesia: arms boycott of, 109; Chinese minority in, 120; commitment to postballot peace, 83; covert special forces from, 16; East Timor

independence, effect of, 130–131;
East Timor security responsibilities,
12, 32–33; East Timorese
Consultative Commission, 69; electoral observers, 88; elections (1999),
29, 53–54; 5 May Agreements,
11–12, 29, 33, 121–122; human
rights violations, 17–18; integration
of East Timor, 16, 20–21; invasion
of East Timor (Dec. 1975), 16; Law
7/76, 16, 21, 79; manner of consultation, 27–28; migrants to East Timor
from, 20; observer delegations, 42;
Portuguese talks with, 18–19; press
freedom limits, 48; prodemocracy
advocates, 35n19; Sunday poll, 46;
voter registration extension, 60;
voter registration objection, 61;
voter registration postponement,
45–46
Indonesian army (TNI): accountability
of, 38; campaigning by, 49; disarmament, 77; INTERFET coordination
with, 114; intimidation of voters, 43;
neutrality of, 31; paramilitary relations with, 25, 44, 48, 56, 82, 84;
peace commission, 29; ransacking of
house by, 47; restrictions on movement by, 71–72; security arrangements, 32; special autonomy proposal role for, 27; troop strength, 71;
violence by, 96; voter registration for
members of, 58
Indonesian Association of Muslim
Intellectuals, 22
Indonesian National Human Rights
Commission (Komnas HAM), 25,
30–31, 70
Indonesian police, 31, 43, 44, 47, 49,
56, 62–63, 71, 72, 77–78, 80, 87–88,
89, 90, 95, 96
Indonesian Task Force for the
Implementation of the Popular
Consultation in East Timor: briefing
in Maliana, 76; campaign code of
conduct, 62; central count, 88; establishment of, 42; media campaign, 47;
paramilitary violence, 83; security
arrangements, 49; UNAMET dossier
on agreement violations, 44; voting
result announcement, 93–94
Integrated Mission Task Forces, 126

Integration Struggle Troops (PPI), 73,
77
Internally displaced persons (IDPs): in
the Dili UNAMET compound,
98–100; militia violence as cause of,
45; numbers of, 45; in the postballot
period, 81; registration as voters,
57–58; in Suai, 75, 77, 92, 96;
UNAMET demands on behalf of, 49
International Committee of the Red
Cross (ICRC), 96
International Federation for East Timor,
56
International Force for East Timor
(INTERFET): arrival in Dili, 114;
Asian participation, 113; Australian
position, 103, 108–109, 112–113;
British Gurkha participation, 113;
Chinese position, 104, 111, 120;
Indonesian position, 97, 104–106,
108–109, 111–112; leadership of,
112–113; participants in, 109;
Portuguese position, 103, 105, 109,
113; Russian position, 104, 111, 120;
Security Council mandate for,
112–114; speed of deployment,
128–129; TNI coordination with,
114; U.S. position, 33
International Monetary Fund (IMF),
107
International Organization for
Migration (IOM), 38, 59
Ireland, 88
Irian Jaya, 123
Isaac, Leandro, 31, 70

Japan, 39, 109, 114, 130
Joint campaign proposal, 63–64
Journalists, 12, 48, 92–93, 98, 106

Kadalek, Hodu Ran, 97
Kamra, 46
Komando Resort Militer Wiradharma
164 Dili (Korem), 99–100, 125
Komnas HAM. See Indonesian National
Human Rights Commission
(Komnas HAM)
Kopassus, 71, 76, 96
Korea, Republic of, 112–113
Korem. See Komando Resort Militer
Wiradharma 164 Dili
Kosovo, 12, 104, 109, 119–121, 129

Kostrad, 94, 98, 100–101, 110
KPS. *See* Commission on Peace and
Stability (KPS)
Kriegler, Johann, 61

Laksaur, 24
Lopes da Cruz, Francisco, 43, 69
Lusophone group, 120

Macau, 16
Malaysia, 109, 113, 120
Mandela, Nelson, 74
Marker, Jamsheed, 13, 91, 123; appointment as Personal Representative, 18;
consultation with Gusmão, 124;
DPA support for, 38; Gusmão move
to house arrest, 74; Indonesian opposition to international force, 97; militia attacks, 26, 93; peace commission, 30; polling day inspections, 89;
security arrangements, 12, 33, 75;
special autonomy proposal, 22; visits
to East Timor, 20; voter registration
postponement, 45, 49
Martin, Ian: appointment as Special
Representative, 37, 40; campaign
code of conduct, 62; consultation
with Gusmão, 124; Indonesian commitment to postelection peace, 83;
militia activity, 48; MLOs, arming
of, 39; opening of voter registration,
54; paramilitaries in West Timor,
115–116; polling day, 89, 91; role in
East Timor of, 12–13; UNAMET
briefing with Tarmidzi, 76;
UNAMET evacuation, 98–100; voter
registration postponement, 45,
48–50; voting results announcement,
94
Mati Hidup Demi Integrasi (Mahidi), 24
Matignon Accords (New Caledonia), 21
Mau Hodu, 97
McKinnon, Don, 107
Media: attacks on journalists, 12; limits
to freedom, 48; voter information
campaign role, 55; voter intimidation allegations, 92
Megawati Sukarnoputri, 33, 105, 123
Mengko, Rear Adm. Yoost, 77
Militias. *See* Paramilitary groups
Mills, Alan (Australian police commis-
sioner), 39, 40, 48, 56, 80, 89, 90,

100
Muis, Col. Mohamad Noer, 76–78, 82,
93–94, 96, 99–101
Muladi, 82, 96, 104

Namibia, 105
Nascimento, Bishop Basilio do, 68
National Council of Timorese
Resistance (CNRT): campaign code
of conduct, 62–63; campaign offices,
63, 75–76; election observers, 89;
establishment of, 19; 5 May
Agreements, 122; flag used as ballot
symbol, 62; paramilitary attacks on,
25, 34n12, 75–76; Popular
Consultation, 84; security arrangements, 32; transitional autonomy, 23;
UN consultation with, 124;
UNAMET demands on behalf of, 49;
voter registration extension, 60;
voter registration of IDPs, 58
New Caledonia, 21
New Zealand: Core Group, 130; international force, 107, 109; standby
military forces, 103, 113; voting
observers from, 88
Nobel Peace Prize, 17
Nongovernmental organizations
(NGOs), 13, 17, 47, 88; voter registration, 56, 58

Office for the Coordination of
Humanitarian Affairs (OCHA), 38,
115
Organization for Security and
Cooperation in Europe (OSCE), 119
Osorio Soares, Abilio José, 44

Pam Swakarsa, 46–47, 49
Paramilitary groups: CIVPOL finding
of weapons cache, 44; disarming of,
33, 68, 77; Indonesian supplying of,
25, 44, 48; international concerns
over, 26; intimidation of voters, 43;
names of, 24; parades by, 73; roadblocks, 49; U.S. report on violence
by, 77; voter registration disruption
by, 56; in West Timor, 115–116
Peoples Consultative Assembly (MPR),
21, 23, 28, 29, 69, 80, 115, 123,
125–126
Perelli, Carina, 40, 91

Pérez de Cuéllar, Javier, 23
Philippines, 109, 112–113
Police, Indonesian, 49, 71, 96
Political prisoners, release of, 20
Pope John Paul II, 106
Popular Consultation: announcement of
   the result, 11, 93–94; appointment of
   special representative for, 37; ballot
   counting, 90, 93; CNRT position, 84;
   Code of Conduct for Participants,
   62; Electoral Directions, 54; flags
   used as ballot symbols, 62; Habibie
   desire for, 30, 130; necessity for,
   121–122; polling day, 89–90; preparations for day of, 87–89; registered
   voter totals for, 60; vote counting,
   88, 92; voter information campaign,
   55; voter intimidation hearings,
   91–92. See also Voter registration
Portugal: administrative authority for
   Timor, 17; East Timor as overseas
   province of, 15; East Timorese
   Consultative Commission, 69; 5
   May Agreements, 11, 33, 121–122;
   Indonesian talks with, 18–19; international force, 103, 106; manner of
   consultation, 27–28; observer delegation, 42, 62, 88, 98, 100; peacekeeping operations, 33; security
   arrangements, 32–33; special autonomy proposal, 26–28; Sunday poll,
   46; UNAMET funding by, 39; voter
   registration in, 61; voter registration
   postponement, 45
Postballot period (Phase II): Indonesian
   contingency planning for, 82, 86n5;
   internally displaced persons in, 81;
   UN contingency planning for,
   79–81, 126–127; UNAMET evacuation, 97–101; violence in, 94–97
Prendergast, Kieran, 40, 85, 105
Prisoners, 58
Public information campaign, 55, 87

Ramos-Horta, José: Dare II meeting,
   68; international force, 106; Nobel
   Peace prize award, 17; return to East
   Timor, 28; security arrangements, 32
Rape, 45, 96
Refugees, 20, 82, 116, 125
Regional Popular Assembly, 16–17
Revolutionary Front for an Independent

East Timor (Fretilin), 15–16
Rezaqul Haider (Chief Military Liaison
   Officer Brigadier, Bangladesh), 40,
   71, 76, 80, 100–101
Robinson, Geoffrey, 86n5, 125
Robinson, Mary, 110
Roth, Stanley, 33
Ruak, Taur Matan, 73, 77
Rwanda, 121, 127

Sampaio, Jorge, 106
Samuel, Tamrat, 13; Commission on
   Peace and Stability, 70–71; consulta-
   tion with Gusmão, 124; East Timor
   leaders meeting, 69; Gusmão
   release, 106; as head of UNAMET
   Jakarta office, 40; human rights, 29
Santa Cruz cemetery massacre, 17–18,
   25
Security arrangements: Australian posi-
   tion, 33; failure of, 48–49, 75–76,
   125; Indonesian responsibility for,
   12, 32–33; Portuguese position, 122;
   UN position, 31, 37; U.S. position,
   33
Serbia, 119
Sexual slavery, 45
Silaen, Col. Timbul, 56, 78, 84, 89
Singapore, 113
Soares, Domingos, 43, 70
Sohn, Bong-Scuk, 61
Spain, 88
Special Autonomous Region of East
   Timor (SARET), 27, 79
Special autonomy proposal, 11, 19,
   26–28, 125
Srebrenica, 121, 127
Suara Timor Timur, 55, 64n3
Subianto, Lieut.-Gen. Prabowo, 23
Suharto, 16, 18, 22
Support Group, 129
Suratman, Col. Tono, 26, 56, 76, 81
Syahnakri, Maj. Gen. Kiki, 78n7, 100,
   114

Tanjung, Feisal, 22, 48, 82
Tarmidzi, Agus, 42, 76–77
Tavares, João, 25, 70
Tetun, 55
Thailand, 113–114
Tim Alfa, 24
Tim Saka, 24

Timor Gap, 20, 34*n1*
Timor Lorosa'e, 131
Timorese Democratic Union (UDT),
15–16
Timorese Popular Democratic
Association (Apodeti), 15–16
Timorese Social Democratic
Association (ASDT), 15
TNI. *See* Indonesian army (TNI)
Transitional autonomy, 23
Tripartite talks, 19, 26–29, 31–34, 75,
79–80, 83, 115
Türk, Danilo, 105

United Front for East Timor Autonomy
(UNIF), 62–63, 89, 91
United Kingdom, 103, 109, 113, 120;
Core Group, 130
United Nations Charter: Chapter VI,
113; Chapter VII, 113–114; Chapter
XI, 15
United Nations Civilian Police
(CIVPOL), 71; advisory role for, 31,
33; carrying of weapons by, 39;
expansion of, 80; paramilitary
attacks on, 95; paramilitary weapons
cache uncovered by, 44; preparation
for voting, 87, 89; recruitment of,
42, 50*n5;* redeployment of, 115;
training for, 41
United Nations General Assembly:
Resolution 37/30 (1982), 18; Special
Committee of Twenty-four
(Decolonization Committee), 16, 18
United Nations High Commissioner for
Refugees (UNHCR), 45, 58
United Nations Mission in East Timor
(UNAMET): authorization of, 39;
campaign code of conduct, 62; commitment to consultation process of,
123–124; concern over danger to,
85; Dare II, 68; disarmament agreement, 78; establishment of, 11,
39–42; evacuation of, 97–101; headquarters flag-raising, 40; internally
displaced persons, 57–58; intimidation of staff, 47–49; humanitarian
affairs officer, 38, 45, 47,
81–82killing of staff, 90, 102*n2;*
local staff recruitment, 41; Maliana
office attack, 47–48; military liaison
officers (MLOs), 38–39, 50*n6,* 73,

94, 97, 115; opening of voter registration, 53; political affairs officers,
40, 43, 81, 97, 123–124; polling day,
90; postballot attacks on, 92; preparation for voting, 87–89; proposal
for, 37–38; protection of civilians,
128; redeployment of, 114–115;
regional campaign committees, 63;
registered voter totals, 60; report on
agreements violations, 44; voter
information campaign role, 55; voting result announcement, 94
United Nations Security Council: emergency postballot briefing, 92; 5 May
Agreements, 11, 37; INTERFET
mandate, 112–114; international
force, approval by, 104–105; international force meeting, 110–111;
Kosovo, 120; mission to East Timor,
100, 101, 105, 110–111; paramilitary
violence, 48, 84; Popular
Consultation, 11; rapid intervention,
need for, 128; Resolution 384
(1975), 17; Resolution 389 (1976),
17; UNAMET postballot restructuring, 80; UNTAET mandate, 115;
voter registration, 49
United Nations (UN): Commission on
Human Rights, 18, 115; Department
of Political Affairs (DPA), 38, 40,
126; Department of Public
Information (DPI), 40; Electoral
Assistance Division, 28–29; non-
recognition of Indonesian annexa-
tion of East Timor, 17; Office for the
Coordination of Humanitarian
Assistance (OCHA), 115; peace-
keeping operation, 33; postballot
period, planning for, 79–81; security
arrangement proposal, 31; West
Irian, 123
United Nations High Commissioner for
Human Rights, 38, 110
United Nations Transitional
Administration in East Timor
(UNTAET), 102*n6,* 115, 128
United Nations Volunteers (UNVs), 38,
42, 80, 115
United States, 33, 83; authorization of
UN missions, 39, 81, 113;
Congressional visit to Suai, 77; Core
Group, 130; Indonesian stability as

interest of, 120; INTERFET, 113; special autonomy proposal, 22; UNAMET funding by, 39
University of East Timor, 41

Van Walsum, Peter, 105
Vendrell, Francesc, 13; consultation with Gusmão, 124; East Timor leaders meeting, 69; political support by, 40; Security Council mission, 105; UN assessment mission, 28–29
Violence: after the vote announcement, 94–97; Alas (Nov. 1998), 20; Baucau killings, 20; best- and worst-case scenarios for, 126–127; campaign-period, 75–76; Catholics as targets, 96, 106; CNRT offices, attacks on, 75; Dili attacks on pro-independence leaders, 25, 70; end-of-campaign militia rampages, 76; Indonesian threats of, 81; journalists as victims of, 12; Liquiça attack on humanitarian convoy, 47–49, 51*n11*, 58; Liquiça church massacre, 25, 30; Maliana attacks on students, 75; Maliana police station massacre, 96; Maliana UNAMET office attacks, 47–49, 51*n11*, 94; Oecusse massacre, 96; on polling day, 90; questions provoked by, 12; Santa Cruz cemetery massacre, 17–18; students, attacks on, 75; Suai church, 77, 96; TNI responsibility for, 124–125; Viqueque UNAMET threat, 47; while awaiting polling results, 92
Voter registration: eligibility, 54–55, 57; extension requests, 60; of IDPs, 57–58; Indonesian position, 49; for military forces, 59; numbers, 57, 60; opening of, 53–55; paramilitary disruption, 56; postponement of, 45–50;

of prisoners, 58; UNAMET role in, 11; of West Timorese, 56–57, 59–61. *See also* Popular Consultation
Voting methods, 28

Wanra, 46
West Irian, 123
West Papua, 123
West Timor: mass evacuation to, 116, 125; Mau Hodu disappearance from, 97; paramilitaries in, 115–116; registration of voters from, 59–61; vote fraud by residents of, 56–57
Wimhurst, David (spokesman and head of public information, Canada) 40, 48, 93
Wiranto, Gen., 91; commitment to post-ballot peace, 83, 122; disarmament, 70–72; dispatch of additional police by, 48, 71; failure to stop violence, 125; international force, 105, 108, 110–111; international pressure on, 83, 108; military liaison officers, 38; militia attacks, 93; peace commission, 30–31; peacekeeping operation, 33; special autonomy proposal, 22–23; UNAMET evacuation, 100; visit to Dili (12 July 1999), 48; visit to Dili (5 Sept. 1999), 96–97, 104; visit to Dili (11 Sept. 1999), 101, 110–112; voter intimidation allegations, 92
Wolfensohn, James, 108
World Bank, 107–108, 126
Wortel, Johannes, 40

Ximenes, David, 41

Yayasan HAK, 56

Zacky Anwar Makarim, Maj. Gen., 42, 46, 76–77, 82, 84

About This Publication

This unique inside account traces events in East Timor from the negotiations that led to the May 1999 agreements among Indonesia, Portugal, and the United Nations to the mandating of international intervention to check the violence that wracked the country following the elections.

Ian Martin, the UN Secretary-General's Special Representative in East Timor at the time, describes how political change in Indonesia, coupled with the UN's good offices and pressures from Australia and elsewhere, led President Habibie to offer the East Timorese a choice between autonomy within Indonesia and full independence. His discussion of what followed—the activities of the UN mission (UNAMET) established to implement the ballot, in the face of violent efforts to coerce the East Timorese to reject independence; the election itself, with a historic 98.6 percent turnout and a 78.5 percent vote for independence; and the ensuing killing, destruction, and forced displacement—includes an analysis of the intense negotiations that led to the Indonesian government's reluctant acceptance of intervention.

With the benefit of his firsthand experience, Martin considers whether the UN was wise to proceed as it did despite Indonesia's refusal to cede responsibility for security during this period and also places the experience in East Timor in the context of the wider debate over peacekeeping and international intervention.

Ian Martin was Special Representative of the UN Secretary-General for the East Timor Popular Consultation and head of UNAMET. He has also served as secretary-general of Amnesty International and has worked for the UN and other international organizations in Haiti, Rwanda, and Bosnia.

Other International Peace Academy Publications

Available from Lynne Rienner Publishers, 1800 30th Street, Boulder, Colorado 80301 (303-444-6684), www.rienner.com.

Rights and Reconciliation: UN Strategies in El Salvador, Ian Johnstone (1995)

Building Peace in Haiti, Chetan Kumar (1998)

Greed and Grievance: Economic Agendas in Civil War, edited by Mats Berdal and David M. Malone (2000)

The Sanctions Decade: Assessing UN Strategies in the 1990s, David Cortright and George A. Lopez (2000)

Peacebuilding as Politics: Cultivating Peace in Fragile Societies, edited by Elizabeth M. Cousens and Chetan Kumar (2001)

Sierra Leone: Diamonds and the Struggle for Democracy, John L. Hirsch (2001)

Toward Peace in Bosnia: Implementing the Dayton Accords, Elizabeth M. Cousens and Charles K. Cater (2001)

Civilians in War, edited by Simon Chesterman (2001)

Peacemaking in Rwanda: The Dynamics of Failure, Bruce D. Jones (2001)

Kosovo: An Unfinished Peace, William G. O'Neill (2001)

From Reaction to Conflict Prevention: Opportunities for the UN System, edited by Fen Osler Hampson and David M. Malone (2002)

The International Peace Academy

The International Peace Academy (IPA) is an independent, nonpartisan, international institution devoted to the promotion of peaceful and multilateral approaches to the resolution of international as well as internal conflicts. IPA plays a facilitating role in efforts to settle conflicts, providing a middle ground where the options for settling particular conflicts are explored and promoted in an informal setting. Other activities of the organization include public forums; training seminars on conflict resolution and peacekeeping; and research and workshops on collective security, regional and internal conflicts, peacemaking, peacekeeping, and nonmilitary aspects of security.

In fulfilling its mission, IPA works closely with the United Nations, regional and other organizations, governments, and parties to conflicts. The work of IPA is further enhanced by its ability to draw on a worldwide network of eminent persons including government leaders, statesmen, business leaders, diplomats, military officers, and scholars. In the decade following the end of the Cold War, there has been a general awakening to the enormous potential of peaceful and multilateral approaches to resolving conflicts. This has given renewed impetus to the role of IPA.

IPA is governed by an international board of directors. Financial support for the work of the organization is provided primarily by philanthropic foundations, as well as individual donors.